LIFE
ACCORDING TO GRANDPA II

Also by John Reseck Jr.

Nonfiction

Marine Biology

Marine Biology Lab Manual

SCUBA Safe and Simple

We Survived Yesterday

Kayak qualification and testing manual

(For the US Coast Guard - Not a public book)

Life According to Grandpa I

Fiction

(Amazon eBooks)

The Man Who Died Twice

The Invisible Assassins

The Cow Blood Case

Coming soon

The Steel Trilogy

The three Steel mysteries
and other short stories
in one Book

Also published in

Skin Diver, National Geographic, Readers Digest,
Kayaker and The Voice Magazines

LIFE
ACCORDING TO GRANDPA II

MORE OF

The Wisdom and Philosophy
of
TOMATEOTS
aka
The Old Man At The End Of The Street

JOHN RESECK JR.

Copyright © 2019 John Reseck
All rights reserved. No part of this publication may be reproduced or transmitted, in any form for any purpose, without written permission of the author.

ISBN – 978-0-999-5620-2-4   printed
ISBN – 978-0-999-5620-3-1   eBook

Book formatting by Connie Shaw
Cover art by: Bruce Berglund

Acknowledgments

A special thanks to

Diane Gnewuch

Karin Crilly

Marge Dieterich

Shelly McGrew

For their help with this project

DEDICATION

This book

Has been written

Specifically for my grandchildren,

But, being well mannered

Children, they will

Share it with

You.

John Reseck Jr on his first backpacking trip, I wonder what he discovered

I love you all,

Grandpa John

Table of Contents

*A*cknowledgments	5
*D*edication	7
*F*orward	11
*I*ntroduction	13
*M*y Diving Life	15
*B*oats, A Major Tool In My Life	37
*P*hotography	59
*M*artial Arts	65
*T*eaching School	73
*B*ike Riding/Racing	81
*A*ntarctic Expedition	87
*T*he Coast Guard Auxiliary	99
*E*xercise	109
*E*pilogue	113

*F*ORWARD

Volume I of *Life According to Grandpa* is a collection of short stories from around the world, taken from my travels and life interests at various times during my 80+ years. This book, *Volume II, discusses how and why I got involved in each discipline, what I learned while there, and what is important to who I am now.*

My life has been a quest for what I could do well. When I was very young, I remember someone asking me, *"Are you ready?"* I don't know what they were asking about but I remember my mothers' answer. *"Johnny was born ready, all he has to do now is find out what for."* I have come to realize I spent my entire life trying to find what it might be.

It has been and continues to be a journey filled with excitement, soul-searching, love, turmoil, and wonder, with each quest teaching me lessons about life. Now, when I meld it altogether, I find that the bottom line for me is, *Reason and Logic* are necessary to get me from point A to point B, but only my *Sense of Wonder* ever gets me to a place I have never been before.

Join with me, as you read about my, *"Pursuit of Happiness,"* in our land of *"Liberty"*.

All I can say up to this point is, *"Wow what a ride!"*

(Many of the photos are scanned copies of 50+ years old newspapers or photo albums).

Introduction

HOW TO LIVE ACCORDING TO GRANDPA II

I have chosen to write about the areas/disciplines that were of major importance to me in my life. Diving, teaching, boating, and the Antarctic are, along with many others, on the list. I will separate each area as much as I can, but of course each discipline supports the others and produces a synergy that has formed the realities in my world. We all live in our own personal world, which we create in our mind. It is my belief that, "*Our past doesn't predict the future, but it does act as a* **prophecy** *as to how we get there.* **It is up to us as to where we end up.**"

In the beginning.

Being an only child, I was born at a time when most people were poor, at the end of the depression in the 1930s, when everything you needed seemed to be rationed. During World War II our family was composed of – a father who worked as a mechanic in Los Angeles because his farm failed to produce enough money to support his family, and a mother whose job it was to keep a husband, son, and herself, happy and healthy, with very little money – you might think, I could have been deprived. That would be a mistake.

I thought I was rich. I was told as a child, by my mother, that we had the gold of the sunset to spend and the sunrises every morning to start us on one more special day. She always had a full meal on the table for us, and the love we had for each other filled our souls.

Everyone I knew was poor, but as kids we didn't know it. Life was just the way it was. Wasn't it the same for everyone? I realize now how hard it was for my parents, struggling to create a good home life for each other and especially for their only child. They succeeded. I grew up having all the food, clothing and shelter I needed, along with *the love and encouragement every child deserves.*

I was constantly reminded by my mother as I grew up that I could be anything I wanted to be, even president of the United States. Thank God, that never happened; it would have messed up my entire life. She and my father imbedded in my brain that to *work hard, respect everyone you meet, and help others whenever possible.* It works.

My parents were not overtly religious, but they lived by the golden rule, "Do unto others as you would have them do unto you." It may not get you into heaven, but it will give you a good life – it did for them, and has helped my life to be full and exciting with many friends I hold dear. *It is a pleasure and an honor for me to share with you some of the what and why of my life's journey, as a* **wonderer**.

A WONDERER AT WORK. HOW DOES SHE DO THAT?

1

My Diving Life

I was fortunate to have been born and grow up, in Southern California during the 1930s and 40s. The ocean, with its beautiful white sand beaches and great surf fishing, was close to where we lived. There was almost no one on the beach we called, "Tin-can beach" It is now called Huntington Beach State Park, and it was free.

About once a month our family would meet a mile north of town at an old oil derrick, collapsed in the surf line. We parked right on the side of coast highway, only a couple hundred feet across the sand to the water. There were usually about eight to ten of us, all sitting around a big camp fire on the beach, eating our supper, which we brought with us from home. We came on Fridays. Each branch of the family came after work, so it was dark by the time everyone got there, but our Coleman kerosene lanterns made a bright spot on the beach for us.

The men took their surf fishing gear, baited up, waded out into the surf, cast out behind the breakers, and waited for a fish to smell the tasty morsel they had on the hook, and make the mistake of trying to eat it. Fishing was good in those days and we normally caught enough fish for several good meals in the next week or two. Fish were an important part of our depression diet, and we fished often.

It was on one of our fishing trips, when I was ten years old, that something happened to set me off on a new path that changed my life. Being a wonderer, *I wondered* what some boys were doing a little way down the rock jetty that we were fishing on. (The story is in "Life according to Grandpa-Walking with the Lions").

The boys were divers and spear fishers. I walked down the jetty and looked at the fish they had, (my dad and I had none), and was hooked, or perhaps I should say, I got the point. They told me about the equipment I needed and how to make a mask and a spear. I was so excited about what I had just learned that I ran back to my parents on the jetty and couldn't stop talking. My mom and dad always supported me in my ever-changing endeavors and said they would help me build a mask and a spear.

I saved the money I earned by mowing the lawns of my neighbors, and bought a pair of 'Church Hill' fins, (Snorkels weren't around yet), made a spear and I started killing fish. I was able to even give fish to the families of my friend who were always happy to get it. The fish was cleaned and filleted before I gave it away - it was ready for the pan. Most of them didn't know how to clean a fish.

On my first dive with my new Church Hill fins, (I was 11 by then), I almost died. My mother, bless her heart, was frightened of the water and never learned to swim. My new endeavor scared her to death. When I asked her to take me to the breakwater in Newport Beach to try out my new fins by swimming along the rock jetty, in case I got a cramp, she had what seemed to be, at the time, a good idea. She would tie a line to me and walk along the rock jetty as I swam along it, "Just in case something went wrong". I said OK, just to relieve her fear, after all what could go wrong?

It was working fine; the line didn't bother me swimming along the jetty. My mother's fear was greatly relieved as she held the line, walking along the jetty, watching me slowly swimming and diving down to look under the rocks. I worked my way to the end of the jetty where there was a large layer of kelp, growing from the rocks, spreading out on the surface. It was beautiful, and new to me. Straining to see what was under its shadow through my mask, I could make out fish, just hanging in the water in the shade. I dove down, (only about 10 feet), to swim under the layer of kelp with the intention to come up on the other side.

My mother, seeing me disappear under the canopy of kelp freaked out. Deciding I needed help, she started pulling on the line, which was now under the kelp canopy. I was trying to come up on the other side as she was pulling me down. It scared me - and her. Later she decided that I didn't need her help to dive, and I learned diving is not a passive sport; you have to pay attention to everything. It was my first real lesson in *situation awareness.*

I also learned that kelp doesn't grab you or pull you down, like all of the self-appointed experts that had never dived falsely believed. Kelp is actually the diver's friend, if you treat it like a friend and don't try to plow through it. It is home for many of the marine animals; and I have even rested in the water on top of it on occasion.

The realization that there was so much about diving that I needed to know, just to be safe, and so much more to know to fully enjoy what I encountered on each dive, led me to a new path of *wonder and study*, fulfilling my dream of becoming a diving instructor with the National Association of Underwater Instructors, (NAUI), and academically a marine biologist. I spent 30 years teaching diving and an appreciation of the ocean environment to a marvelous group of young people, mostly at Santa Ana College, (SAC). I signed well over 5,000 certification cards, *which were their personal passports to sharing my land of wonder.*

Because of the diving program I had going at SAC, the publisher Prentice Hall asked me to write a text book to be used in SCUBA classes across the country. The book, *'SCUBA Safe and Simple'*, became one of the main diving texts in the 1970s and 80s, and still sells as a history book on how diving used to be. Even today it's a good/fun read for any diver.

As a board member of NAUI, I was sent to oversee instructor classes on the campuses of the University of Hawaii, Texas A&M, and Simon Frazer University, in Canada. I also served as director or staff member on twelve other instructor courses. I taught diving and underwater photography classes on the campuses of UCI, UCLA, Fullerton State, as well as several community colleges.

I am very proud of the fact that I was inducted into the NAUI Hall of Honor, and share that with Cousteau and others that I have great respect for in the diving world.

I wish I knew who those boys were on the Los Angeles breakwater that cold winter morning 70 some years ago, that took the time, as they shivered in the cold, to share their world of wonder with that little kid, that had so many questions. I would love to say, "Thank you".

Some of the lessons I learned during my diving years,
And how I learned them.

- Will you sponsor our club?
- If you say you can't, you're right.
- Be sure you ask the right questions.
- When it takes skill and knowledge – practice.
- Don't assume all is well–especially with your buddy.
- Teaching someone a rewarding life skill is as good as it gets.

What diving did for me.

- It financed me through seven years of college.
- It opened up the writer's world to me.
- It led me to a lifetime of wonder.
- I made incredible friends.

Will you sponsor our club?
Why and How I Became a Diving Instructor

When I started teaching biology at Santa Ana College in California, (my credentials are in biology, oceanography, physical sciences and education), the word got out about my diving. The school paper did an article on me, like they did on all new teachers. It told my story of working my way through seven years of college as a commercial diver, among other things. Some students approached me and asked if I would sponsor a dive club for them. Of course, I said, "Yes", and was excited to have a reason to get back into the water.

I went to the administration to start the procedure to establish a new club on campus. I was surprised at the response - it wasn't positive. All they could talk about was the liability exposure. I finally convinced them we would allow only certified SCUBA divers to dive with any gear other than mask, fins and a snorkel. It was a hard sell, but at last they said OK. It was then, I realized, I wasn't a certified diver; it was 1965.

All of the 1,000+ hours I had under water was done either as a commercial diver, or on my own with friends. The sport diver's certification card was a fairly new thing. You got one by taking an 18-hour class taught by a dive shop. I could not very well require the students to need a certification to join the club, if I didn't have one myself. I went to my local dive shop and signed up.

The class taught me some very important things that I really needed to know, not about diving, but about the skill level of a newly certified diver. Everyone I was used to diving with was strong in the water. The people that shared my diving class with me, and got certified, along with me, scared me to death. Most of them could hardly swim and were told that was all right - they didn't need to be good swimmer to be a SCUBA diver. I couldn't believe it. I had at that time, 20 years of diving experience, and I knew that things go wrong in the water, just like every place else once in a while, and the diver had to **calmly** solve the problem. Panic in the water becomes a life and death situation very quickly, not a 911 situation. Looking at my twelve fellow students, now certified, I could see panic, if they encountered a severe equipment failure, like happened to me on several occasions. Bottom line, *I didn't feel they had the watermanship skills to be safe divers.*

The class was as good as it could be in 18 hours, but didn't come even close to what my standard was to be a safe diver. *I made a decision; I needed to become a diving instructor and teach my students myself.* I went back to my administration.

This time it was an easy sell because I was selling safety. I put together a PE class called, Free diving. It ran 16 weeks with two hours in the pool a week. I figured with 32 water hours I could bring their watermanship up to a safe level, then teach about shallow water-blackout, and enough about the mammalian reflex to make them decent breath-hold divers.

Now the question came up - did I have the qualifications to teach a diving class? Not on paper, and the fact that I could free dive to 100 feet, and had all those years of experience didn't count. In our society you always seem to need, "the paper." The administration said, "Get certified as a diving instructor and it's a go." I found an instructor's course that was being held during that summer (1966) at UCLA and took it. The class was certified by the National Association of Underwater Instructors, (NAUI). I had no idea what it would be like. I assumed it would be like a normal college class like I was used to teaching – I couldn't have been more wrong.

I knew the class was nine days long, we would be living right there on campus, and I *was* to bring my diving equipment. That was the extent of my knowledge of the class and NAUI. I went to Mexico for a week, on a diving trip with my friends and came directly back from there to UCLA.

At the registration desk there were two people in front of me and overhearing their conversation, I knew I was in trouble.

They were worried that they didn't have enough reference books to study. I joined in the conversation and met my first two classmates. I had never even heard of most of the books they had. They were all books on teaching sports diving with SCUBA gear, the medical considerations and the physics of diving. I hadn't read any of them, and I found out I couldn't buy them there.

There were about 40 of us in the class and I was the only one that had no idea what was about to happen. We were rousted out of bed at 6:00 am every morning and never stopped moving until 10 at night. We were either swimming in the pool, giving graded talks in a class room, swimming and diving in the ocean, taking notes in a lecture, taking written tests and finishing at 10pm every day. Then we studied for an hour or two for the next day's testing. Every thing we did was graded. This was a week of testing us to see if we had the knowledge and the skill needed to be a NAUI instructor, not to teach us those skills. I didn't even know what it was I was supposed to know and be good at.

I had to get certified. I had a class at the college, filled with students, waiting to be taught when school started again. I took a deep breath and dug in. I borrowed some books and read well into the nights. I got up at 5:30am and swam in the pool to get my swimming without fins back on track, so I could pass the swim test. I failed it the first time it was given, (a quarter mile, in ten minutes). One of my fellow candidates was a swim coach; he coached me, as I swam, every morning, at 5:30, for five days and I finally made it.

I was fortunate that most of what I had to know, I already knew from my experience and my biology and physics background. What I needed to do was organize, in my head, how it all went together in the diving field. I ended up helping some of the others in the areas of physics and diving medicine. It was an intense and scary week for all of us, I will never forget it. I was destined to, over the years, participate in 15 more just like it, but I was the one giving the test, so it wasn't scary at all.

The club was responsible for guiding me onto a whole new path. It blossomed into a major club on campus, with 60 members by the end of the year. All of them had taken my free diving class as well as a SCUBA class some where else. I went back to the administration and sold them on the idea that we needed a basic SCUBA class.

It only made sense to increase training to assure student safety. They were taking an 18 or 20-hour course and the one I was planning was a 60-hour course. It was 16 hours of lecture, 36 hours training in the pool, plus four ocean dives, two from the beach through the surf and two from a boat. The increased safety factor for the student was obvious and the decreased liability probability for the college was, too. They said, "yes".

In order to inform the community about the diving program, I gave talks/programs to any group of people I could find. Service clubs, church groups, high schools, people at a signal waiting to cross the street - no one was safe from my message. I gave over 200 programs in two years, many times two a day.

During the next seven years the program grew. Lectures had over 100 students in them We employed four more diving instructors and had the largest program in the country that we knew of. In its final stage, it included eight separate diving courses, and certified over 10,000 students in various classifications, even 25 new diving instructors. It is worthwhile to note we had no major accidents during the 18 years the program was offered.

IF YOU SAY YOU CAN'T, YOU'RE RIGHT.

The students were some of *my* best teachers over the years. There was always one that would say or do something that enlightened me and gave me new insight *into my life*. In one of my early diving classes a young woman was the first to demonstrate to me, *how our brain controls our ability to perform*.

The first thing I had every student in all the diving classes do was a swim in the pool with no fins. I wanted to see if I had a potential panic victim that I needed to pay special attention to. I had them swim across the pool and back, only 50 meters, but far enough for me to see if they were comfortable or not in the water with no equipment to help them. I felt this was very important in case they have an equipment failure in the future.

One of my students in the free diving class was a heavyset woman and it was her turn to swim. She told me, "I can't swim that far". I knew because of her build that she would float really well. I told her she could swim right next to the side of the pool and could grab the side if she couldn't make it. I would walk along the deck with her. I knew she could make it because she couldn't sink.

She started out doing a breaststroke/dog paddle and was moving right along. She reached the other side, pushed off and was in no stress at all as she came back across the pool. Four feet from the finish she suddenly stopped, took hold of the side of the pool and said, "I can't make it". She wasn't even breathing hard. It was a revelation to me. I had trouble even comprehending what had just happened.

She had told me, and her brain was listening, "I can't make it." So of course, the brain, that controls every move we make, wouldn't let her make it. It taught me to listen carefully to what people say, because it tells me what *limitations they have put on themselves*. Be very careful what you say, because your brain is listening, and wants to make sure you're not telling a lie. Never limit yourself, use your full potential or you will never know what you are really capable of. **Never say, "I can't"**.

BE SURE YOU ASK THE RIGHT QUESTIONS.

Fifteen years after the start of the dive program at the College, one of the earlier students came back to the pool to visit. I had seen her on and off during those 15 years and had always asked if she was still diving. She always told me yes. She had a boy friend that was a diver and they went on trips and dove whenever there was water to dive in.

Our class was going on a weekend trip to Baja California, Mexico, to do the final two dives for their certification and she asked if she could join us. I said she could, knowing she had been diving for the last ten years since she finished our class at the College.

We arrived at the campground on Punta Banda, set up camp, and the students made a SCUBA dive with their dive masters. There was one of my assistants to dive with each buddy pair. The next day, on their final dive, the students would dive on their own with a buddy of their choice. Our visitor didn't dive that first day because we were very structured and she didn't really have anyone to be her buddy.

The next day I was the odd man out and wanted to make a dive to look for a type of shell that I knew was in that particular area. I ask our visitor if she would be my buddy. She said yes. We had a spare tank for her and I had a set of double tanks. Making a mental note that she would run out of air before I did, we entered the water. I watched her for a few minutes and she was relaxed and doing fine. I started looking for my shell and she swam along close to me. We were in 30 feet of water for the first ten minutes, then came to a drop off that went straight down to 90 feet. I wasn't finding my shell in the shallow water so I dropped down to the 90-foot level.

We went through a thermocline at 50 feet and the water temperature dropped about five degrees to 54 degrees. I could feel the cold-water seeping into my wet suit. The water was crystal clear and visibility was a good 100 feet. I turned to check on my buddy to see if she was alright. She was calmly hanging suspended in the water right behind me with her arms hugging her chest. She was feeling the cold water, too.

Starting to turn around and begin looking for my shell, I realized she was a little heavy and had to keep using her fins to keep from sinking. The wet suit compresses as you get deeper, due to the increased pressure, and loses bouncy so the diver has to put more air in their bouncy compensator (vest) they wear to balance themselves out to be in a neutral state again.

I was also aware of the amount of time we had at 90 feet without decompression and it wasn't very much. In our dive because of the shallow dive we did first it was going to be about 15 minutes. I swam back to her so I could blow some air into her vest to save time. In those days we put air into the vest by taking the SCUBA mouthpiece out of our mouth and blowing air into the vest through a small tube right under our chin. I didn't want to waste time having her do it.

I swam rapidly up to her and took my mouthpiece out as I approached her, grabbed her harness, gently, pulled her close to get to her vest, and blew some air into it. I backed off and checked her buoyancy and she was fine, then I realized she didn't have her regulator in her mouth, or in her hand. It was hanging down behind her, "OH MY GOSH" I thought, "SHE IS OUT OF AIR DOWN HERE AT 90 FEET."

I swam back, grabbed her harness, this time really not gently, pulled her up tight to me and stuffed my regulator in her mouth, so she could breath, then headed for the surface. I kept the regulator in her mouth all the way to the surface, while I made a free assent, carefully monitoring my exhalation.

Expecting a big thank you for this heroic act that I had just successfully executed, saving the life of a damsel in distress, I was shocked by the first words out of her mouth, when we broke the surface, *"That was a rude thing to do!"* What in the world, had just happened?

I hadn't asked the right questions. When I asked her if she had been diving all those years and she had said," Yes", she was telling the truth, but it had been free diving, not SCUBA. The last time she had a SCUBA tank on her back was on her certification dive with our class, 15 years earlier. She said that when she saw me swim up to her, and take my mouthpiece out of my mouth, she remembered me saying, in class. "If you see a fellow diver and their regulator is out of their mouth, assume they need to start buddy breathing.

What she didn't remember, was me saying, *"Never lose control of your regulator, you control the buddy breathing by feeding them air". When she saw me swim up with no regulator in my mouth, she just spit hers out for me to use. I had not seen that, and she couldn't find it hanging down behind her. She also forgot how to do that.*

That lesson has saved me a lot of embarrassments over the years. First of all, I don't assume as much as I used to, and if it is something important, I ask several questions, not just one

When It Takes Skill and Knowledge – Practice

There are many situations in diving that take both specific knowledge and skill to execute safely. Normally, there is time for the diver to work through them at a slow pace, however, if there is an *equipment failure*, there may be no time to think about how you are going to solve the problem. It has to be an automatic reaction. As a commercial diver I thought out a procedure for everything I could think of that could possibly go wrong and practiced my solution until I was proficient doing it.

I was on a dive to collect Angel Sharks for an aquarium. The ones we were after averaged four feet long and were resting on the sand bottom, covered with sand. We caught them by grabbing their tail with one hand and putting the other hand in the middle of their back so they couldn't bend back and bite us in the face. I was working on a shelf 100 feet down. This was in the days before the single hose regulators and I was using a two-hose regulator that had just been rebuilt. We did a lot of deep diving and had our regulators checked on a regular schedule.

Everything was working fine as I swam down to the bottom and started my search for a shark. I took a few breaths and there was a little water in my air intake hose. I thought I had just let it in around my mouth and went on with the dive. A few minutes later I exhaled and started to inhale. The entire hose was filled with water, no air.

My situation was dire – I had just exhaled, I knew I couldn't make the surface before I blacked out. My training kicked in, I knew the tank had air in it and I knew that the regulator released air from the tank whenever the pressure at the mouth piece was lower than at the regulator. That is why divers could get air from the tank - they sucked on the hose, the pressure was lowered in the hose and air was released for them to breath in through their mouth. I turned over on my back making the regulator on the tank deeper than the mouthpiece so the air would free flow out of it, which was standard procedure for clearing water out of the air hose. I tried breathing again, the hose was still filed with water. I started for the surface, now holding the mouth piece high over my head to increase the pressure differential between the mouth piece and the regulator. That action made a greater pressure differential between the mouth piece and the regulator and the tank released air in a continuous flow. It was bubbling out of the raised mouth piece. I brought the mouth piece down low enough that I could suck enough air out of the stream of bubble, to make the surface.

My knowledge of the equipment I was using, coupled with the fact that I had practiced breathing out of the air bubble stream just for fun, saved my life. One of my favorite sayings is, "Knowledge and skill will get you from point A to B, but only a sense of wonder will get you to points unknown". In this case I was very happy just to get from point A to point B. We found that the regulator was working fine, it was the rubber hose that had a split in it. When I turned my head to look around, it stretched the hose and water rushed in. Practice all safety procedures as much as you can. When you need them, they have to be automatic. One other thing is important, remember - practice doesn't make perfect, it just makes what you practice the way you will do it. <u>Only perfect practice makes perfect.</u>

Don't Assume All Is Well – Especially With Your Buddy.

The perfect story for this is in Volume I of my memoirs in the diving section. It is called "The Scary Cave", I will give an abbreviated version of it here. We were diving on a coral reef off the coast of Cozumel, Mexico. The water was clear to 150 feet and warm at 82 degrees. Perfect conditions and all of the eight divers, were very relaxed, and just drifting along on a beautiful night dive. The moon was full and bright; I fantasized I was drifting through space in the twilight of a wonderful dream.

My buddy and lifelong friend, Dick, were diving together in shallow water at 30 feet, when we came onto a cave in the reef. During the previous few days, we had dived these caves many times in the daylight. They had holes in them and the bright sunlight had filtered in so you could see very well all around. Dick motioned to me, that he was going to enter it. I decided to stay out of the cave, turn off my light, and enjoy my moonlight fantasy on the reef. It was a place I had never been before

Time passed and my buddy hadn't come out of the cave. My air was starting to run low and I knew his would be, too. I decided to signal for him to come out. I turned on my light and shined it through one of the holes in the top of the cave to get his attention. Seeing it he came to the hole, took his tank off, keeping the regulator in his mouth, and passed the tank out to me, as he squeezed himself through the small hole, cutting his shoulders on the coral.

It turned out he had been lost in the cave, trying to find a way out for the last ten minutes, and he was running out of air. He was on the verge of panicking. I had assumed he was just fine and almost let him drown. If you are a diver, remember your buddy's life is in your hands, and, even more important to you, is that your life may be in theirs. Choose your diving partner very carefully, and never neglect them.

Teaching someone a rewarding life skill is as good as it gets.

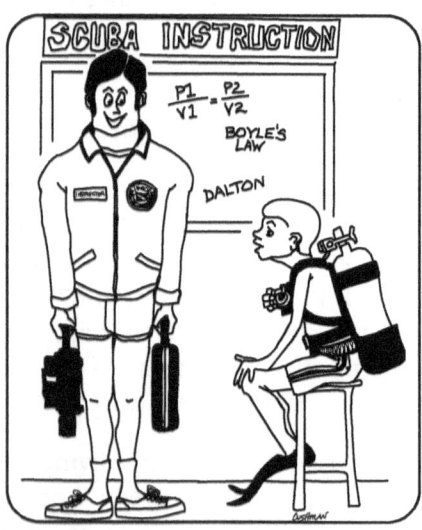

Teachers of any subject teach because they want, whoever they are teaching, to be aware of something they need to know or will make their life in some way better. It is a simple concept. The thing that makes most teachers special is that they rarely get solid feedback about the difference their teaching had on their students, but they still continue to teach. We all assume we are doing a good job, and that our students are better off because of what ever it is we taught them. It is rare, however, to ever get confirmation of that.

I had the opportunity to teach Driver's Training for a few years to high school kids. I loved it. At that time, it was the only thing I taught that gave me an immediate feedback from my students. In just a few weeks they went from a non-driver to driving on the freeway, and doing it safely. Teaching diving was much the same for me. When I signed their card, I knew they had the tools to be a safe diver. The difference was I didn't know if they would keep diving or not. It took years for that information to filter back to me.

During my active years as a diving instructor, (1966-2002), I made many friends of my students. One of them, Jeff Bozanic, gave me the compliment of introducing him into the NAUI Hall of Honor. Three other students, joined me on the record setting kayak trip, down the coast of Baja California, Mexico, (the book, "We Survived Yesterday).

Several of my past students heard I was back in town. I had been living in Washington state for 18 years after I retired, and they contacted other past students that they knew, and hosted a party for me. There were 20 people there. I have no words to express how incredible it made me feel. They were still diving, and It had become an important part of their lives.

Since I have returned to California to live, I have been taken to an abalone dinner, (Thank you Steve Wright), and been invited to a fish fry, where I visited with old friends, (Thank you Steve Markusic). I don't think of them as old students any more, they are my friends.

I gave one of my books, a Marine Biology text I wrote, to a young high school girl that said she wanted to be a Marine Biologist, and now she is, with a PhD degree. I have had several students from my Self Defense classes call me over the years, and thank me for a certain skill I taught in class that got them out of a bad situation. I have come to realize that to teach someone a skill or anything that they can use in their life to make it better, is as good as it gets. *I want to thank all my 15,000+ past students for giving me the opportunity to make my life both interesting and worthwhile.*

What Diving Did For Me.
It Financed Me Through Seven Years of College.

As I was growing up, it never occurred to me that I could go to college. Out of 14 uncles and aunts, I had one uncle that I knew went to college, and I knew my parents didn't have any money to send me. In high school I took all of the math, physics, and biology courses that were available, because I liked them and did well in them. I didn't realize that I was taking a college prep track of courses.

My mother was a high school graduate, and my father only went to the fourth grade. That was as high as the one-room school on the farm went, in 1906. He was my shining example of what a good man was; he had provided for his family well and as I grew up, I figured I would just follow in his footsteps, where ever they led me.

In the 10th grade I made a decision that literally changed my life, without even knowing it. I was throwing the shot-put on the high school track team, and not doing very well. I decided to try football. They practiced after school, and that was fine. I rode my bike to school, and time didn't matter.

I found that an old farm boy could be pretty good at football. Each year the city of Los Angeles picked the best high school players in each position and created an honorary all city team. I made the team all three years in high school, as a left tackle. I was happy about that, but my mother was ecstatic when I was offered a full scholarship to UCLA. I had a B average and was good to go. Her dream was that I could go to college. She never talked about it, because it seemed impossible.

I started UCLA in the winter of 1953, was there only two months, came down with pneumonia, and had to drop out of school. Of course, I lost my scholarship. Should I go back to my original plan? I had loved my classes at UCLA and decided that one way or another, I was going to go to college.

My dream job growing up was to become a teacher. If I went to college, I could fulfill that dream. My two months at UCLA had relieved me of the fear of college that had worried me as a farm boy. All I needed now was Money.

I had friends that were commercial divers and I talked to them about how I could use my diving skills to make money. With their help, I worked over the next eight years as an abalone diver, a sea urchin diver, a hard-hat diver fixing moorings, and as a diver putting on the underwater show for the glass-bottom boats in Avalon, on Catalina Island. Diving produced 80% of my total income for the entire time, (seven years) I was in college.

THE UNDERWATER SHOW FOR THE GLASS BOTTOM BOATS WAS MY MAIN JOB. I WORKED ON THE BARGE FOR FIVE SUMMERS

The other 20% came from being a bouncer in several bars, (by this time I had taken a third place in the national YMCA judo championships), and doing anything I could, that I got paid for. I cleaned bathrooms at night in several hotels and cleared weeds off of vacant lots on weekends. My photography helped me along also, working in the college photo lab between classes. No job was too small. It took seven years to get my Bachelors and my Masters, along with a lifetime teaching credential. College was a series of one wonder after another. It was a great time in my life. I never did play football again. By the time I was physically able to, I was so deep into my new academic life, I didn't have time to, *but I appreciate the fact that the only reason I went to college was football, and the only way I could afford to go, was diving.*

IT OPENED UP THE WRITER'S WORLD TO ME.

My book, Scuba Safe and Simple, was published in 1975 and it opened a whole new world to me. A gentleman visited me in my office at the college, and asked if I would consider writing a text book for diving classes. He was representing Prentice Hall publishers. I asked, "Why me?" He said, "You are running the largest diving program in the country, you must know how to teach it". I told him that I was honored to be asked, but I wouldn't have the slightest idea how to write a book. In 1973 he came back again, and I declined once more. In 1974 when he came and asked me again, he said the magic sentence, "Do you realize you could make a lot of money with a SCUBA text?" That caught my attention.

What he didn't know, no one else did either, was that I had mild aphasia. What is that? Well, it is a brain disorder that impairs the memory of words. My handicap was that I couldn't picture words in my brain to write them down on paper. I had to sound out almost every word I wrote, and it would be misspelled 60% of the time. It also made me a slow reader - how could I write a book? I told myself there must be a way to mitigate my handicap, (there were no computers then to help me out).

Through college I avoided all English classes possible, and in science and math classes I very seldom had to write anything. I knew there must be a way. One of the secretaries at the college that knew of my problem - she had been typing my tests for many years and we would laugh together at some of my spellings. I asked if she would type what I hand wrote, (I didn't type), and I would pay her so much a page. She agreed and I had my solution to putting it on paper. Now what and how should I write was still a mystery to me.

I had written several articles for Skin Diver Magazine, and became good friends with Paul, who was the publisher. I called him in Los Angeles and asked if he would have lunch with me, I needed some advice. He agreed and met me a few days later. I told him my situation - that I didn't even know how to start to write a book. He told me, "Just pretend you are talking to one of your classes". He had been to some of my classes. He said, "*Don't try to show everyone what you know, like most writers do; just make sure that they know what they need to know.* Use your stories and jokes as if you were in class, and they were right in front of you. The book will be a winner".

I took his advice, sat down at my desk, and over Easter vacation, when no one else was around, hand wrote the entire book in nine days. My secretary friend typed it up and gave me a complete copy to edit. I read it through, made a few changes and hired another professional to type a new copy. I gave that copy to Prentice Hall, and waited for their reaction.

It was very positive. They sent me a ticket to fly back to New Jersey, and sit down with their final editor, just to make sure they put it all together the way I wanted. The book, *SCUBA Safe and Simple,* was a big success. It made me a lot of money, and launched me into an entire new world that I had never even dreamed possible for me

When they asked me, the next year, if I would write a Marine Biology text, I asked the same question I had asked before, "Why me?". I was no expert in that field. They said the reason the SCUBA book did so well was because of the way it was written, they wanted the same style in the

Marine Biology book. I said I would. That book took me 18 months to write. I had to check every word I wrote, to make sure it was correct and that it was what the student needed to know. I was not the expert in that field, but like the SCUBA book I just pretended I was talking to one of my marine biology classes. It was a bigger success than the SCUBA book. I was now an author, and very financially successful. I have written eight more books since then, and none of them have made much money. I think that means that I have finally, truly, become a writer, and like most everything else, I just did it in reverse.

It Led Me To A Life Of Wonder.

All children are born with a sense of wonder. They wonder about all the new things they encounter as they are growing up. What an incredibly interesting path they are on, everything in their life, is new to them. As we grow older, and learn more about our surroundings, we tend to lose the desire to wonder. Wondering takes a great deal of time and energy, and there is always some thing that uses up both our time and energy that seems more important to us. We evolve into a life of familiarity and routine, and become comfortable. The older we get the fewer new things are there for us to wonder about, if we accept our life just as it is. Diving changed that for me, every dive presented me with new wonders to investigate and learn about. I was never satisfied with what I knew. It didn't frustrate me, it just made me a more aggressive wonderer.

The only way for me to answer my own questions of what, why and how, was to become a marine biologist, so I did. A life as a scientist is basically a life of wonder, because we never find the final answer to anything. Every new thing we find out, or discover, just creates more questions. The quest for knowledge never ends, it just expands. It has been an exciting and fulfilling life for me. I have come to realize that like Sargent Schultz, of the old TV series, Hogan's Heroes, said, "I know nothing", but I sure, for 84+ years, have had an exciting and fun time trying to learn everything.

I Made Some Incredible Friends. Forward

Diving, like any field, I suppose, has a cadre of people at the top that are leaders, and usually wonderers. Being the diving officer at Santa Ana College, I was privileged to be accepted into their circle, and made friends with some of the most interesting and intriguing people from several countries. They became my role models as well as friends and still play an important part in my life, well into my retirement. I am sure that when each of them reaches the *Pearly Gates,* they will swim in leaving a wake and ask," Is there good diving up here?"

2

Boats, A Major Tool In My Life

I use the word tool because that is what all of my boats have been to me, something needed to do a job. That changes the way I look at them from the normal way most people do, as a fun thing to enjoy leisure time. The boat is in reality, a tool for them also - it helps them stay sane in today's environment, which is quite crazy at times. The only thing that is more demanding of your time and money is an airplane. The boat at least is up front about it, the word BOAT stands for, "Break Out Another Thousand."

As I ponder and evaluate the boats I have owned, used or rented, and include the kayaks, I can count 29. Only three or four of them were used solely as pleasure boat, just to have fun in. I see a boat as a device that lets you move across the water to some place you want or need to go. It also is a tool that will let you live on the water. I did that several times. I have had many jobs that required a boat to do them, or perhaps, I got the jobs because I had the tool to do them. In any case, boats have been a major tool that has helped to shape and define my life. My self-image includes the fact that I was a boater.

I am only going to list the boats I have skippered and the work they did for me. It is a wide variety of styles and types. Every mechanic knows that you need the right tool, if you want to get the job done - I learned that from my dad.

My first boat was my dad's. I was only six years old when we got it. It was a *12-foot-long rowboat, made out of sheet Masonite*. It remains the only boat I have ever heard of that was constructed out of Masonite. We had a 5hp outboard for it. My dad bought it in 1941 to fish the local lakes. He bought it used so I have no idea how old it really was. He never used it, but I did. I learned how to row a boat and became quite skilled with the oars. In 1949 I used it to set long lines off of Newport Beach and sold the fish I caught to my friends' families.

It's only claim to fame happened when I was 17 years old. I took it to Catalina Island with a washing machine in it. I was going over to the island for the summer and took a small washing machine to Avalon. The room I had rented for the summer had been a basement until they put toilet down there, then it became my apartment. I learned a lot about a compass on that trip. It was only 26 miles, but I did it in dense fog. I used a boy scout compass on the floor at my feet, almost missing the island. When the island became visible to me through the fog, it was less than a mile away, but it was the wrong end of it, still 20 miles from Avalon. It was almost as far as when I started. I had to buy more gas at the Isthmus to get to Avalon. I decided It was time to take a Coast Guard Navigation class.

I built my first kayak when I was 18. I saw one at Catalina and ask the man in it where he got it. He told me where to get a kit to build one. I found the ad in National Geographic and built my first *Folbot kayak*. I used it for a few years to dive out of, then broke it in half, one day in the surf.

Jan and Dave packing their boat in preparation to paddle to Cabo San Lucas, from Shelter Island in San Diego California–1,200 miles. (Book, "We survived Yesterday")

Over the years I have had *9 kayaks*, but never more than 7 at one time. Each one did something special. They were the right equipment, to do the job at hand. Some folded so I could take them in an airplane, some were for rivers and some were for open ocean travel. **I loved them all because they took me to places, and adventures, that I couldn't' get to any other way.**

In 1950 my dad bought our first power boat, the *"Sea Eagle"*. It was 26-feet long and had a gas engine in it. The albacore were running right off shore a mile or two and he wanted to commercially fish them. We rigged it with two long poles, one on each side called, 'out-riggers", attached trolling lines to them, and went to sea. We caught fish and made a small amount of money, but he found he got sea-sick, and that ended that endeavor. I however, had learned how to rig the commercial lines and got a summer job on a boat out of Catalina Island that caught a lot of fish. I saved my money. It gave me a good start when I decided to go to college.

The second summer I worked in Avalon, on Catalina Island, I was hired by Al Hanson, the hard-hat diver that checked the moorings in Avalon Harbor. He was looking for a diver to put on an underwater show, in a hard-hat rig, in the aquarium tank he had in the middle of town. It was a huge tank, eight feet deep and 27 feet in diameter. I took the job and learned how to dive in a full hard-hat rig. I had made a displacement helmet out of an old water heater when I was in school, but Al's rig was a real hard-hat commercial suit.

The suit had a face plate that shut and locked in the front of the helmet, a 30-pound breast plate, a 30-pound weight belt and 10-pound foot weights. The air came from a compressor on the boat, through a hose, and was a steady stream into the helmet. The diver had to control the amount of air in the suit by pushing a valve in the back of the helmet, with his head. Too much air in the suit and the diver became too buoyant, too little and they got suit squeeze. When Al thought I was competent in the tank, he took me on his boat, the *Jenny*, to work on moorings in the harbor.

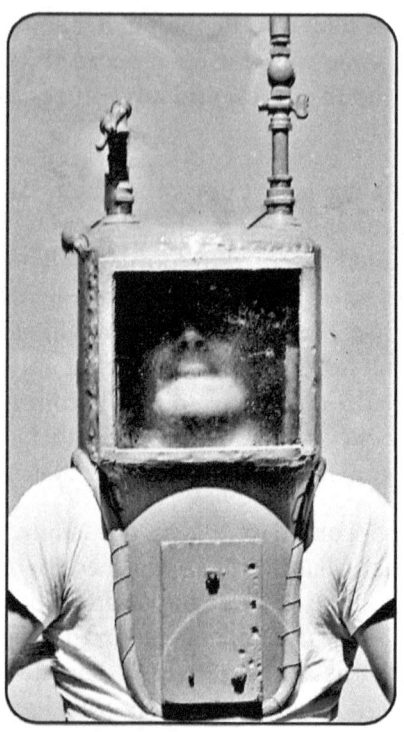

My first hard-hat I made myself out of an old water heater. My father had a welding rig at home. It was a displacement type helmet. It worked as long as the diver didn't bend over, and the man on the surface kept pumping air.

There were just the two of us on the boat, one to run it and one to be in the water diving in the hard-hat rig. That was a very scary situation for me. He went in the water, and I had to manipulate the boat to follow him, tend his diving lines and not get my prop tangled up in them or in the mooring lines that were everywhere in the water. He put his life into my hands. If I screwed up at any of the chores, he would probably die. I was 18 years old, scared to death the entire time he was in the water. Then, after an hour he came up and it was my time in the suit, and my life at risk. We traded off, working the deep water first, to avoid the bends. I worked for him one entire summer and neither of us died.

At the end of that job, I was asked, by Harold Warner, who was in charge of the underwater shows for the Glass Bottom boats, if I would put on the shows under the Glass Bottom boats, the next summer, in SCUBA gear. I said, "Thank you God," and jumped at it. I would be working off an anchored barge with aquariums on it, instead of a moving boat with my air supply dependent on a hose in the water close to a spinning prop.

When I got the diving job putting on underwater shows for the Glass Bottom boats in Avalon, my boss had a 27-foot boat, *the Green Dolphin*, and I ran that for five summers. We collected specimens for the aquariums on the dive barge. We went out before the shows started in the morning or after work, to keep fresh animals in our six large aquariums. The *Green Dolphin* was a fast boat and a different design than I had run before. I was getting to understand how the different hull designed changed the way the boats handled.

During the years I worked on Catalina I rented some place to live in Avalon most of the time. There were a couple of periods when I had a job there, but couldn't find a place to rent, so I commuted from Los Angeles Harbor, in whatever small boat I had at the time, until a rental came up.

The distance across the Catalina Chanel was about 23 miles from the place in Los Angeles harbor where I launched my boat. The boats used at different times included a 13-foot runabout, a 12-foot and a 16- foot inflatable and a16-foot runabout. All of them were outboards. I only had to sleep in the little boats, tied to the dingy dock in Avalon, about a dozen nights because the water was too rough for me to get back to the mainland after work. In the morning it was always calm enough for me to get to work on the island.

In 1966 I was going through a divorce and needed a place to live. My banker, who lived on a boat with his wife, said there was a couple who lived on a 40-foot Block-Islander-Cutter sail boat, and were looking for someone to live on their boat and take care of it and their dogs, two standard poodles, while they took a one-year cruise as teachers on the College- at-Sea ship. I jumped at the offer and moved on the boat with the two dogs. It was the first time I lived on a boat in a slip, as my home. I loved it.

Several things happened that year. I learned how to train two giant poodle dogs, and when to reset my priorities.

The two dogs ran to the bow of the boat every time someone walked along the dock, and barked and growled at the poor person just a few feet away. They were used to doing it and the people that lived in their boats put up with it, but I wasn't going to. I had a Red Rider bb gun with just enough power to sting, but not enough to break the skin. I kept it in the cockpit of the boat, and every time the dogs attacked someone I would shout, "No", and shoot them in the butt. It only took two times and they stopped it. They would run up to the bow, I would say no, and they would come back to the cockpit and go back to sleep.

It was while I was living on the sail boat that I made what I now consider a major mistake. The boat was in Newport Harbor, just a hundred yards from John Wayne's house. Every morning I walked the dogs past his house. One morning I was in front of the house when he came out, in his bathrobe and slippers, to pick up his paper. He was right there by me so I said, "Good morning, John." He looked up, and I could tell he was trying to place me. I said, "I was going to say, good morning Duke, but I don't know you well enough to take that liberty, I considered Mr. Wayne, but I know you too well for that, because I've seen so many of your movies. The only thing left was John." He broke out laughing and invited me in for a cup of coffee. I declined, saying that I had a class to teach at the college at eight o'clock. I can't believe I turned down a chance to have coffee with John Wayne. It's my fathers' fault, he's the one that taught me my work ethic. I have regretted it ever since. When a once in a lifetime opportunity pops up, reset your priorities and take it. I could have called in and canceled the class.

I LOVED LIVING ON THE BOAT, AND EVEN WROTE A POEM ABOUT IT.

My Friend the Bay

Each day when I awake, I look out at the bay.

Each day it says," Good Moring."

Some days it is calm and bright and

The greeting is "GOOD MORNING."

Other days it is windy and rough and

Its "Good Morning" is almost sarcastic.

Once in a while I find it hiding in the fog.

I try to cheer it up but it will not speak.

I guess we all need solitude

Once in a while.

When the time came for me to move off the sail boat, I bought a 27-foot Chris Craft, the *"Todo Tiempo"*, and moved onto it. I lived on it for a year and a half. I rigged it to carry SCUBA tanks and used it as a dive charter boat. With my six-pac Coast Guard license I could transport five divers to Catalina and back. I made the trip every Saturday and Sunday, for a year.

THE MAS TIEMPO

That worked out so well that I sold it and bought a 32-foot Luhrs, the "Mas Tiempo", and lived on it. It to was rigged to use as a charter, but I could still carry only five divers. That was the limit on my license, but it was a much bigger boat for me to live on, and it opened up a different type of charter for me. Now I could take four people on multiple day charters. I even took several two months charters into the Sea of Cortez. On these trips Steinbeck's' book about his experience in the Sea of Cortez was always available. He loved it too.

On one of the Sea of Cortez trips, the engine overheated on the trip back up the coast, on our way home. We stopped, turned the engine off and I checked in the engine room to locate the problem. It wasn't hard to find. The fan belt had broken. I had a spare but it wouldn't fit because the alternator had frozen up and the pully would not turn. The full story is in volume I, but the lesson learned was to expect the unexpected. We made new belts with the rubber bands on our spear guns, and with the help of the crew and their machine shop, on a Japanese Tug boat, made it home.

I was into living on boats now and wanted a bigger one. Trading my 32 foot in for a 55-foot converted Coast Guard Buoy Tender, I got what I wanted; it seemed like I was living in a mansion.

THE LINDA LEE

I didn't charter the "Linda Lee" for dive trips because it was only an eight-knot boat and wasn't fast enough to charter to Catalina. It was my home. During the next couple of years, I took it into the Sea of Cortez twice, for my entire three-month summer vacation. On these long trips, I took my wife, dog, and two student deck hands, who paid for the fuel on the trip. A cheap way for them to have a great three months.

We had a dive compressor on board and dove every day. We started at Newport Beach and motored down the west coast of Baja, around Cabo San Lucas, and up the east coast of Baja, diving all of the islands and the Baja coast to Mulege – then we dove all the way back to Newport Beach. They were fantastic trips. Between all of us on board we would make an average of 300 tank dives, and at least as many free dives, each trip.

I lived on the *Linda Lee* for four years and only moved off of it when the dock doubled our slip rent if the boat was lived on. With the extra money it would have cost me to live on it, I bought a condo near the college, and leased the boat to three friends for the next three years, finally selling it.

I was without a big boat then for a few years, but I still had my inflatables, kayaks, and even a canoe. I used these in my summer classes of marine biology and the desert survival that I was teaching for Santa Ana College, in Baja, Mexico.

In 1984 I applied for and was given a one-year sabbatical leave, from Santa Ana College, to collect shore-line marine specimens from three different environments, for use in the College biology classes. The areas I chose were the Sea of Cortez, the Florida Keys, and the inland passage of the western Canadian coast. *I needed another boat.* This one needed to fit on a trailer, big enough my wife, Sharon, my dog, Drifty and me to live on at sea for three months at a time. It also needed enough deck space to do my work of preserving and identifying the collected specimens. A search was initiated for a boat that would do all those things.

It was found on the cover of a boating magazine. I saw a picture of a new make of boat. The one in the picture was the first one ever built. It was called a C-Dory and it was built in Washington state. It was 22-feet long, had a small stand-up cabin and a large cockpit. It had two engines, a 50 hp to run it and a second, seven and a half hp, outboard for trolling when you were fishing. For us the smaller engine would be our safety engine - we were going to be in strange places and it would be a stress reliever to have a second engine. A few phone calls later I located that exact boat that was on the cover, in Nevada at Lake Mead. It was for sale. My wife and I drove five hours to Lake Mead to look at it. It met all our needs to do the sabbatical. We drove back home to Santa Ana. The next weekend we drove back to Lake Mead, with our Bronco, and bought the boat.

Our rig for the year,
nine months at sea and three months in the camper.

We were ready now. We had the Bronco, with a camper on it, to pull the boat across the country twice, down to the Sea Cortez and back home from Canada at the end of the expedition. We would live in the camper when we were traveling on land, and in the boat the three months we would be at sea. I had some modifying to do on the boat to fit our special needs. It wasn't designed to live on.

It had a portable toilet placed under the wide end of the Vee Bunks in the bow. To use it at night you had to get up and move the mattress. It was right under your head when you were sleeping. Not satisfactory. I moved it to under the seat that was for the table, next to the door of the cabin, as far from our heads as possible, which was only six feet. On the starboard side of the cabin was the helm and a small sink, but no running water and it drained into a bucket under the sink. If you had water in a container under the sink, you could access it with a hand pump into the sink. On the Port side there was a small table with a bench seat on each end so two people could sit. The portable toilet was under the seat by the door. There were only six-square feet of floor space left in the cabin.

There was no room for a stove of any kind in the cabin, so I built a platform over the outboard engines that we could put a Coleman two burner stove on and cook outside. I constructed an aluminum frame, so my wife, Sharon, could make a sun/rain cover for the back deck, she also sewed a cover for the entire boat out of mosquito netting. We were going to be in bug country in Florida. To complete the modifications, I had two fuel tanks of 25 gallons each fabricated to place in the stern, to also acted as seats. We were ready. We headed out for Baja the first week in January, 1984.

Part one - Baja California, Mexico

Our first three months were to be in the Sea of Cortez, launching the boat in Loreto. We encountered a problem I had not anticipated on my, "what if", list I created when I was planning the trip. Before we launched, we had to fill all of the fuel tanks with enough fuel to last us at least six weeks, to reach our next available fuel in La Paz. I had five six-gallon tanks and two 25-gallon tanks, that when filled, together weighed 600 pounds. When the tanks were filled at a gas station, the boat flattened out the springs on the trailer and rubbed the tires on the frame. I put the small tanks in the Bronco, (that helped a lot, 250 pounds), and the tires still rubbed the frame, but just a little. I only had two miles to go from the gas station to the launch ramp. I drove at five miles an hour and we made it. Scary.

When we launched the boat, I placed the five small tanks on the bow and tied them down to balance the 50 gallons I had at the stern. It worked well. During the voyage, we kept the boat balanced in the water by switching fuel from the tanks, back and forth.

We visited all the islands and coves south to La Paz, then went back to where we started to get the car, and trailer the boat off to Florida. All was going as scheduled and we were getting used to the tiny quarters we were confined to. We had been out for three weeks and were relaxing and enjoying the quiet of a small cove at an uninhabited Island, Isla Santa Catalina, when a cruise ship pulled up and dropped anchor just outside us. We couldn't believe what we were seeing. There were people all standing at the rail looking down at us.

The big ship launched some inflatables and they started carrying loads of "stuff" to shore. They finally came over to our boat and apologized for the disturbance. Their boats, making multiple trips to shore and back, right past us, were rocking our little boat like a cork in rough water. They invited us to join them on shore that evening for a party. We jumped at the chance. It turned out to be much more than just a party for us. We were treated as honored guests and sat with the guides, guest naturalist, and the captain, as well as the owner of the tour company.

The food and cold drinks were a wonderful treat for us after three weeks of living in our "tiny home", but the highlight of the evening was the people we met around the bonfire. A world expert on cactus was there. As I can best recall, his name was Lindsey. I had read some of his work when I was studying desert survival. The author of two of the books that were required reading in my Marine biology class, "The year of the whale" and "The year of the seal", Scheffer, was also there and so was Mr. Lindblad. This was an inaugural trip to the Sea of Cortez for his Lindblad tour company. The conversation was incredible for me. It was a chance of a lifetime that I didn't miss out on.

The funniest thing that happened on the Baja part of our year, happened while we were anchored in La Paz harbor. Sharon needed to use the portapoddy, located under the seat by the door to the cabin. The cabin door, was always open. She had just pulled down her shorts and sat down on it, when a small boat came along side with three young men in it. They were the crew off of a large yacht anchored next to us. They had seen our boat a week earlier 20 miles north and just wanted to say hello. They were on the side of our boat that looked right in the cabin door at Sharon. Sharon couldn't move off the pot, they were sitting in their dingy looking right in at her. We talked for about 25 minutes, and they left. She just sat there like she was sitting at the table and carried on a conversation, they never knew the difference, *but she sure did!*

Part two - The Florida Keys

When we left Baja and drove back home to California, we bought a new heavy-duty boat trailer. The one we had was breaking down because of all of the weight we were carrying on it. It was designed to carry the boat empty, not with an extra 1,000 pounds we had in it. The heavy duty one we replaced it with worked fine clear across the country and back. We lived out of our camper for the week it took us to drive to Florida. When we got to the city of Homestead, we launched and resupplied our boat for the several months in the Keys that were planned. Leaving the Bronco in Homestead, in a secured parking lot, we put to sea again.

Bypassing Key Biscayne, because it was just another city, we went out to Elliot Key and did some collecting for a few days. Our next stop was to be Key Largo. Cruising down the inside route to Key Largo, all was going as planned when the outboard engine started making an awful noise. I shut it down and switched to the small engine. We saw a marina that had a big sign, Marine Mechanic; we pulled into a vacant slip that was right next to the shop. We were on Key Largo.

The mechanic came out, we took him for a short ride, and he said," Your lower unit needs to be rebuilt", telling us it would be $650.00, and take a week. I had no choice, I agreed. He told us we could live in the boat right there in the slip. That sounded good. We discovered, however, there was a problem - we would be living right in a mangrove jungle.

An hour before sunset a cloud of mosquitos appeared, every night, and ate any flesh they could find. Fortunately, I had planned on having a bug problem in Florida and had a bug net that covered the entire boat, so we were safe if we put it on early, which we did, and never took it off for a week. Now the problem was, we were stuck on the boat, looking out at the world through the mosquito net, that had several hundred mosquitos hanging on to the outside, hungrily looking in at us.

We had an interesting, and scary, experience during that week. In the middle of the night we were awakened by a helicopter flying right over our boat, then multiple gun shots going off somewhere nearby. Before we could get out of our bunk, a boat came fast into the empty slip next to us and some men jumped out of it speaking Spanish. I know some Spanish, but they were speaking so fast I couldn't understand any of it. My wife had our dog, Drifty, in her bunk and was holding her mouth shut so she couldn't bark. We didn't want the men to know we were there and could hear whatever it was they were talking about. We didn't know what was said, but they wouldn't know that. In a couple of minutes, they were gone. The three of us went back to sleep.

In the morning, I found the mechanic and told him what happened. He was unconcerned and said they bring drugs in from Cuba all the time and the Coast Guard helicopters chase them. The druggies toss the drugs over the side of the boat if they think they are going to be caught. He said for us to watch all of the fishing boats that will show up today. They drag hooks on the bottom, hoping to snag a bag of the good stuff. He also said the Government was wrecking the Florida economy by cutting down the drug trade. At first, I thought he was making a joke, but he wasn't. Our week finally ended, the boat had an engine again. We took it for a trial run - it sounded just like it did when we brought it in.

The mechanic said, "It must be in the upper unit. I'll have to rebuild it". I had already paid him $650.00. to rebuild the lower unit, (which now was obvious didn't need to be done) I was stuck. I agreed to another $650.00 for the upper unit. He told me it would take one more week to get the parts. I looked around for Sharon and found her around the corner of the building, crying.

I had never seen her cry before. She said, "I don't think I can stand another week cooped up under the bug net, with them crawling all over it calling our names." I knew exactly what she meant and decided to hitchhike back to where we left the car, bring it to the boat, pick her and the dog up, so we could get out of there and live in the camper for the next week. I did that. We were comfortable again in a camp ground, where we actually had flush toilets. We were told that we also had an alligator that roamed the campground at night and to be sure to keep the dog inside. They were telling the truth - it went right by our camper and was a good ten feet long. Our week of luxury ended all too soon, and we drove back to the boat.

This time when we ran the engine, it worked like it should. We motored off down the chain of Keys, (islands), and finished that portion of our year, anchoring off shore every night away from the mosquitos and without any more unplanned adventures.

Part Three – British Columbia

Finished with Florida, we headed across the United States to the Canadian west coast. It was a long drive, and we camped in many camp grounds on the way. We were in Tennessee, I think, camping, when one morning a pickup truck stopped at our camp. An old man, (younger than I am now), came over and looked at our boat on the trailer. He asked me where we were going with the boat. I told him, "Clear to Canada."

He replied, *"Oh good, cuz that boat would splash all the water out of our lakes around here for sure."* He got back into his truck and drove off.

When we got to Montana, we received some bad news. Sharon's sister was in the hospital very ill. Sharon flew back home and I drove on to Canada. Three weeks later her sister passed away, after a lifetime of illness. Sharon rejoined me in Seattle. We then continued on to Vancouver, BC, to launch the boat for the last portion of our one-year adventure, doing field work.

There are many intriguing islands between Vancouver Island and mainland British Columbia. We visited 31 of them during the three months we spent there in the boat. It's a boater's paradise - calm water, (most of the time), and hundreds of little coves for a small flat-bottomed boat like ours to anchor in. We looked for places to explore that most boats could not get into.

We were in just such a place, several miles back in a very narrow fjord, when it became even too narrow for our boat. We anchored our boat, and got in the six foot inflatable that we used as a dingy. I rowed the dingy through the narrow passage, (about 15 feet wide), with Sharon, and Drifty, into an incredibly beautiful lagoon.

It was a mile long and 200 yards wide. The GPS said we were right at 51 degrees of Latitude, in the middle of the lagoon. That marked the top of the area that I had chosen to do my collecting. This was as far north as we were going. It was time to start working our way back to Vancouver, and then the 1,300-mile drive back to the college and to work. It was going to be a big adjustment having to be back on a work schedule again after such a fantastic year of adventure and living on a non-schedule.

After an hour or so of exploring in the lagoon it started to rain heavily. We had rain suits on, but decided to get back to our boat, get into some dry clothes, have a cup of hot chocolate, and enjoy the solitude/wonder land, we were in. *It wasn't to be.*

As we approached the narrow passage to the lagoon, I heard a roaring sound. Not knowing what it was, I decided to put the boat ashore and go look at the passage. Walking a hundred yards to get a good look at it, I was stunned. The calm water that we rowed through to get into the lagoon, was gone. In its place was a five-foot waterfall. The tide had gone out, and the passage was too narrow to empty the lagoon fast enough to keep up. If we had gone over the waterfall, none of us would have survived. The water was a torrent, crashing on the rocks below. I had read about the "reversing waterfalls", in the area but had never seen one of them.

I walked back to the boat, told Sharon that we were going to have to sit on shore for about six hours until the high tide came back in, and then we could row back through the passage. She said, without any hesitation, "**No we're not.**" I was shocked at the determination in her voice, she never talked like that. I was getting ready to explain why we had to wait for the tide to change, when she pointed behind me. There were two very big grizzly bears walking along the shore line toward us, less than a football field away. I just said, *as I was pushing the boat off shore,* "You're right."

We sat in that six-foot dingy in the middle of the lagoon, being battered by the heavy downpour, for five and a half hours, before I could row us back to our boat. Sharon didn't complain, but the dog was really unhappy with me.

I learned a number of things during our 1984 adventure. First, no matter how carefully you plan, it has a high probability of not working out just the way you thought it would. You always need at least a plan 'B', if not a plan "C".

One other thing, I became aware of was how important it is to have a dog that can't talk.

The 200+ specimens, collected on our 1984 exposition, were placed in the *Wet Room* where such things were stored at the college, where all the instructors had access to them, to use in their Biology classes. It had been a great year.

Retirement

In 1990, I retired from Santa Ana College, and moved north to Port Ludlow, in the state of Washington. I still had the C-Dory, but it wasn't a good boat for what I wanted to do there. We had joined the Coast Guard Auxiliary, and needed a boat that I could do official patrols in. I sold the C-Dory, and bought, the, *"Friend ship"*, (with a friend), a 27-foot Bay Liner cabin boat. It was a good boat for patrols.

The way the Coast Guard system worked was very efficient. The Puget sound area was divided into various areas. The Auxiliary boats, (mine, and many others), were assigned to patrol a given area on any given day and keep contact with the main Coast Guard sector via VHF radio every 30 minutes or so. They knew exactly where we were, all of the time. If a boater had trouble on the water, they would call the CG in Seattle, who then contacted the nearest Auxiliary boat to render aid, and to tow them to the nearest safe harbor, if necessary. There was no cost involved to the boater.

After a few years the law changed and we couldn't tow anyone because Vessel Assist took over the towing and charged for it. The boaters weren't happy and neither were we, but what is; is. I bought a larger boat, the "Motivator". It was a 41-foot, tri cabin trawler. I used it to train new auxiliary members to be qualified as crew or coxswains, so they could act as crew on our patrols. I had her for 15 years.

The Motivator

We trained over 100 people on the Motivator. It was an intense training program, and took many hours at sea and classroom to complete. We sold her when we moved back to California, in 2013, and my wife and I retired, after 18 years, from the Coast Guard Auxiliary.

We moved from Port Ludlow, Washington, to Laguna Woods, California, to be near some of our family and closer to medical facilities. The first month after we arrived in Laguna Woods, all of the items we had stored in our storage shed were stolen, including a kayak, along with all of my diving equipment, an inflatable boat, bike, camping gear, and most of my fishing equipment. None of it was recovered.

I got angry at first, then disappointed in my new environment. It is challenging to make something positive out of a set-back like that, but necessary, so you don't get caught up in the "poor me" syndrome. I finally decided that it was my mother, from the spirit world, still taking care of me. I could imagine her saying, *"Johnnie, you're in your 80s now, and you might hurt yourself with all those complex toys"*. Once again, she came to my aid and solved the problem.

Rental Boats

There are times when you need a boat and you don't have the right one in the right place. Easy solution, rent one. My first rental was a 36-footer out of Vancouver, Canada.

It was during the time I owned the C-Dory. My wife and I had just completed the 1984, yearlong trip, and were back to work. I had my summer vacation coming up for three months, but Sharon only had two weeks off. I made a plan, (we'll call this plan A).

I would take the Bronco and pull the boat up to Prince Rupert, Canada. I planned two weeks for that. Sharon would fly up there and meet me. We would spend two weeks together on the water in Alaska, then she would fly home, and go back to work, while I drove the car and boat back. Really very simple.

One of my good friends, said he didn't think it was wise for me to make the drive alone. He offered to make the drive with me. He said then his wife would fly up with mine, and they would stay in our camper and travel around the area for the two weeks, while Sharon and I were on the water. She would fly back with Sharon and he would drive back with me. Made good sense, (we moved to plan B).

Another friend asked, if I could get there a few days before the ladies flew up, he could fly up and fish with me in the boat. His dream was to fish in Alaska and Canada. He would fly home when the wives arrived. I said that would work, (we moved to plan C).

The plan C friend, had a wife, (they were newlyweds), she threw a *"hissy fit"* - " if you go, I should be able to go too." Well, the boat wasn't big enough for more than two on it. The camper on the Bronco, was only big enough for two, so what to do? We had a vote, I lost, it was five to one. We would charter a boat out of Canada and all six of us would fit on it at once, and stay in the Canadian Gulf Islands. There would be no drive to Alaska, and no time for either couple, (A or B), to have the two weeks alone. We rented a 36-foot cabin cruiser for the two weeks, (we moved to plan D). If you think that must be the end to the drama, you would be wrong.

The wife of the plan C friend only had a one-week vacation, and had to fly home from wherever we were going to be at the end of the first week, which meant we had to be in a place that had airplane service - so much for being off the beaten track, (we moved to plan E). When the time came for her to fly home, she had another *hissy fit,* *"why* should he be able to stay, when she can't?" He flew out a few days later to please her. I have not heard from them since. I wonder if they are still married?

THE SOUTH PACIFIC

We rented another boat, and this time, we had a perfect cruise in the Island Country of Tonga. The trip was to celebrate the 70th birthday of one our yacht club members by sailing around the Tonga VaVa'u group of islands. It was north of New Zealand, and east of Australia and was just like posters of south sea islands, a few palm trees on pristine little islands.

We flew to Fiji, had a 12-hour layover, hired a cab and driver to give us an eight-hour tour of his island - changed planes, continued on to Tonga's' main Island of Nuku Alofa, spent the night, then took a flight, several hours north, to the Tonga VaVa'u group of islands. The boats we rented (We had enough people to need four boats, with four people to a boat) were 40-foot Beneteau sail boats. The boats were spacious, and very comfortable. The trip was as perfect as it could have been. Calm seas, good friends, air temperature around 80, water temperature 83, and visibility under water over 100 feet. We spent hours every day in the water with our snorkel gear. It was a dream trip. I would go back in a heartbeat, except it is a long, long way away, and that makes it expensive and a very tiring trip.

KAYAKS

As you can tell, I had a long string of boats, but I always had at least one kayak to go along with the others. I built my first one in 1950, and broke it in half in1955, trying to surf it in waves that were bigger than I could handle. Of course, I didn't know I couldn't handle them, until I broke the boat in half trying.

The only way to find your real limitations is to reach them, *not to create them in your mind.* I remembered what my mother always said, *"The only things you can't do are the things you don't know how to."* I took surf kayak lessons, practiced, and learned two things. First it takes skill and practice, to handle the surf, and second, you don't do big surf in a canvas boat with a light wood frame. I increased my limitations. I built another kayak and used it for years to dive out of.

Much later, in 1991, when I paddled the 1,200 miles down the Baja California coast, my surfing skills were indispensable. There were four of us on that trip, all very experienced paddlers, and we still had two capsizes, one pitch poll, (end over end), and broke one of our Kevlar boats in half, all in the surf.

The two things that stand out during my many years using Kayaks are first, the trip down the Baja coast mentioned in the paragraph above, (you can read about that expedition in its own book, *We Survived Yesterday*, available on Amazon, as an e-book), and second, establishing kayaks as an official program for the Coast Guard Auxiliary to use on official Coast Guard patrols. I wrote the training manuals for the program at the request of the Coast Guard. We initiated it in the North West, and now it is active on the east coast.

We took our kayaks to many different environments; on several occasions we rented house boats to live on. This one is in Lake Powell, one of our favorite places to investigate. Our kayaks were stored on top and we used the houseboat as our mother ship.

WHAT DID BOATING TEACH ME?

Boating taught me to be self-reliant. When your boat has a problem, you had better know how to fix it, especially if you go off shore often, and I did. I became good enough at diesel mechanics to at least get us home when we had problems.

I learned to accept help when it is offered, even if didn't need it. If you keep turning help down when it's offered, people will stop offering it, and the day will come when you need it.

Living on all the different boats taught me that I didn't need a lot of room to live a very comfortable life. If I had a good place to sit, to sleep, to cook, and a desk to work on, I was fine; I had everything I needed. All of the other "stuff" I have in my house now, is just that, *'stuff'*. Even though much of it is out of date or just plain useless, it is still *my stuff*, and very hard to get rid of. It is of great importance that *we create* an exciting future for ourselves, so we don't get bogged down in the past, and start to biodegrade, surrounded by all of our stuff.

SOME BIG FISH SHARON CAUGHT

I also learned caution. I never take a boat out without checking weather. Early on I made the mistake of not checking weather, and got badly beat-up. I check everything now, not just the weather, no matter what kind of trip I am going on.

I loved boating, and like so many of the other components that at one time or another created my self-image, boating, with time, has slipped away. I remember all of my adventures fondly, *but it is the ones that are in front of me, that I have yet to experience, that I am excited about. I can't help, but wonder, what they will be?*

3

Photography

Photography entered my life by way of a comic book. I was 13 years old and reading a comic book on the beach, while I waited for a fish to take the bait at the end of my line. There was an ad that read, "Get everything you need to be a photographer, just $10." It listed, a camera, film, a tank to develop the film, chemicals to use, paper to print the negatives, and a safe light to use in a dark-room. *It said you could do it all at night, in your kitchen.* Now what boy, that wondered how everything around him worked, could resist that offer. I had $10 from mowing lawns, and became a photographer.

I waited anxiously for the package to come. It seemed to take forever. Every day, when I arrived home on my bike from junior high school, I asked my mother, "Did it come yet?" Then one day she was waiting on the front lawn for me, and said, "It did", and handed me the package.

I took it, ran inside, opened it, and spread everything out on the kitchen table. It was all there, with some instructions on how to mix the chemicals and put the film into the camera. There was a small pack marked 'Photo paper". I wanted to see what it looked like, opened it and then read the instructions, "Do not open except in a dark room with a safe light". My photo paper was now useless and turning purple. *It turned out to be one of the best mistakes I ever made.*

I was devastated. I realized I had just ruined my photo kit. My mother told me not to worry, she was sure I could buy more paper at a photo store. There was one on my way home from school that had just opened a month earlier. It was there I met Bill and his wife Marcie, the owners of the shop. They guided me on a path that opened an entire new world for me.

I was so enthusiastic, they hired me to sweep the floors and clean the windows of their store. That gave me the money, to buy everything I needed, as I progressed on my quest to become a photographer. During the next six years, Bill took me in the darkroom and taught me what I needed to know to be a good lab technician. He took me on his photo shoots as his gopher, and taught me composition, lighting, camera angles and use of filters. He was my mentor, coach, and friend.

When it was time for me to graduate from high school, I had worked in the shop for six years, he asked me what I wanted to do for a living? I told him I thought I would go to Brooks School of Photography and become a professional photographer. He told me he wouldn't advise that. I thought he meant I wasn't good enough, I was crushed.

He laughed at me when I told him that. He explained to me he thought that I loved photography so much, it would be a shame for me to have to do it to make money. He told me to make money some other way, and to keep photography as a hobby and avocation. That way, what I loved would never become just a job. I think he was relating to me his relationship with photography. He loved it, that is why he opened the shop. Now after these past years it had become his job, I followed his wise words, and found them very true. I still love the camera and what it can do. Now in my 80s, I find I can still use a camera as well as I ever could, and digital gives me so much more to learn.

PHOTOGRAPHY 61

BULL SEA LION - GALAPAGOS ISLANDS - ECUADOR

In college, my skills in the darkroom got me a part time job in the photo lab. I hired out to photograph weddings and parties. My camera became one of the tools I used to get me financially through my school years.

After I became a teacher, the camera became a tool to illustrate what I was teaching. A picture is truly worth those 1,000 words I had heard about all my life. I taught Biology, and being able to show, as well as tell, the student what I was trying to convey was marvelous. The slides I accumulated over the 30 years I taught were all to illustrate some point or show some trait that was hard to describe. The color slide collection I ended up with was over 10,000 slides. When I retired, I offered the collection to several different schools, and couldn't even give them away. No one uses slides anymore – now it's all digital and projected from the computer.

After I retired from teaching, my wife and I traveled a lot. I was using the camera, taking photos like most tourist do; just general photos that had no particular reason to be taken, except they were pretty pictures. That all changed when my wife passed away.

I found myself in the state of mind that I realized most everyone that loses their mate of many years must go through. I was lonely and depressed, with no scheduled activity of something of substance to do. I needed to reorganize my life in such a way that it moved forward, so I wouldn't stagnate into a biodegrading recluse, sitting in a chair reading, and watching TV all day. At 80, It would have been very easy for me to do.

I sat down and made a list of skills that I thought I was still at least semi-competent in, considering my various health issues. It wasn't a very long list, but photography was on the top, and writing was next to it. Teaching and photography had created a synergy that had improved both for me, in my teaching life; I could see where writing and photography could blend to create the same situation in this new chapter of my life. You might even say it saved my life by opening a whole new world to me to wonder about

SPREAD YOUR WINGS....

THE WORLD IS WAITING.

AFRICA - BOTSWANA

My photos now are used to make wall hangings and photo posters. Sometimes I think of a saying and search for a photo to go with it. Other times I have a picture that I like and it seems to tell me what I should say on it. The posters are a lot of fun for me to create, and I have my house full of my wall pictures.

My mentors, Bill and Marcie Cox, are dead now, but I think they may be smiling down, at the 14-year-old boy, that rode a bike up to their shop one day and asked, *"Do you know anything about photo paper?"*

4

Martial Arts

I am fortunate to have been exposed to a variety of different "Martial Arts." Some of them classical, like Judo, Karate, and Kendo, along with Law enforcement, military, and special forces technical courses. The classical ones were my favorites. They taught a way of living. The physical part was only a factor of the process. They taught physical control, mental stability, and self-reliance. I learned how, and why, mental concentration and focus are so important in our everyday lives. The others were specific techniques for dealing with various types of aggression. Their usefulness was specific to situations not normally encountered by most of us, however they were very important at the time, for me.

Judo was by far my favorite. It was the first one to enter my life. I was a young teenager in search of something I could compete in that would fit into my school and work schedule. I saw a judo class advertised in the newspaper at the YMCA, and jumped at it. The instructor was a Canadian and taught classical Kodokan Judo, along with all of the philosophy that went with it.

He was not only very good at the art of judo, (a second degree blackbelt), but also an excellent example of what all of the martial arts should and, depending on the instructor, teach their students – how to be self-disciplined, self-reliant, and how important it is to focus on what you're doing.

He also stressed that you should never allow yourself to get angry. Once you get angry, you lose focus, and all of your ability is downgraded, both physical and mental. He was emphatic that you should never use physical force unless it is in self-defense. He believed *"The brain is the most powerful weapon you have – train yourself to use it".*

These were lessons that have served me well all of my life. When I became a judo instructor at Santa Ana College, I did my best to teach them to all of my students. They were of highest importance in the self-defense classes, because in those classes I taught how to disable someone – it wasn't a sport. I called it JonBo-jitsu just for fun. It was a combination of all the fighting arts I had been exposed to. My office partner gave me a drawing he said was a visual description of my class.

Judo means *gentle way*, although if you watch a modern competition, there is nothing gentle about it. The moves and throws seem extremely rough, but in fact each throw is designed to land the opponent on their back, and we practiced how to land on our backs constantly. It sounds awful, because of the beat/slapping with our arms we use to break the force of the fall so we are not hurt. One reason I like Judo over the others forms is that, it is full speed. It's the best you can do.

ONE OF MY FEMALE STUDENTS DEMONSTRATES A THROW. WELL DONE.

I taught Judo at my college for 15 years, and loved it. The coaches would have the football linemen take my class. They thought it was helping them with their balance in combat conditions. I hope it did, but I know for sure it helped me to maintain good technique in my throws. Those big linemen were strong and tough. When I worked with them, I had to do the moves right, or get smashed.

There was one funny happening that I still laugh at when I think of it. It was during finals week, when I always gave each student, (there were 25 in each class), a chance to go full speed with me and try to win a match.

I used the old-style Judo line up. My students lined up against the wall with the smallest one, on one end of the line, and the biggest one on the other end. In a real judo competition, it would be the lowest ranking one to the highest ranking one. They would count off by twos, and the ones would be on one side of the room and the twos on the other side. The lowest ranking would be the first in each line, and as the lines progressed, the rank stayed fairly even on both sides. The rule was, if you won your match, you stayed up, and took on the next one in line. You stayed up as long as you kept winning. There was no rest period between matches.

The difference for our final in the class was the entire class was in line one, and I was the only one in line two. The first time I did this, I started at the small end and worked my way up to the big end. After that I got smart and worked from the big end to the small end. My father once told me, "Son, if you have a dumb head your whole body suffers", He was right.

It was after one of these, slaughter lines, as my students referred to them, I went into the coach's dressing room to shower and get out of my white judo clothes. The president of the college was there changing into his running shorts to go for his daily run. He looked at me, took a step backwards, and asked, "What the hell happened to you?"

I looked in the mirror at myself and even I was shocked. My white uniform had blood all over it and there was even blood on my face. Nothing serious, just scratches mainly from finger nails, but quite a few of them.

"I just came from the final in one of my Judo classes" It was all I could think of to say.

"We don't pay you enough." He said. I agreed. He turned and went out for his run but he never did pay me more.

I credit my Judo training to saving my life, twice. I mentioned that a major part of our training was how to fall without injury. I have taken quite a few falls in my life. That training, I'm sure, is the main reason I was never seriously injured, but two of the falls could have killed me, and I walked away from both of them with soreness, but nothing serious.

The first one, I caught my foot on a chain in the bed of a pickup truck as I was going to jump out of it backwards. My feet stayed up in the bed of the truck and my body whipped down on the cement driveway flat on my back. If I had not instinctively tucked my chin to my chest and locked it there so it would not smash on the concrete, I would have died.

The second fall I took when I was 83 years old. I slipped off a log crossing a stream and fell on the rocks of the streambed. My feet went backwards, off the log, and I came down right on my face in the rocky stream bed. I again had practiced, this type of fall during my training. You have no time to think how you are going to hit the ground, it has to be an automatic reaction. If I would have put my arms out to catch myself, I would have smashed my face right on a big rock. It was because I kept my elbows in, and crossed my arms in front of my face, I only got a small scratch on the end of my nose, a close call.

When you practice something for 40 years, like falling, it becomes automatic to do it the best way possible. I didn't realize that my judo training would be of major importance to me when I was an old duffer. *Be careful what you practice, and remember that, only perfect practice, makes perfect.*

THE BEST WEAPON

I had one incident that proved, to me, that the brain is truly your first and best line of defense. While I was working on Catalina Island at night as a bouncer, stacking away money for school, I was asked to do something that seemed at first outside my capabilities. My boss told me to throw out three men that were being foul mouthed and loud. They were giants, all at least six foot six inches tall and big, not just tall.

I checked them out and thought about what would be the wisest thing for me to do. I seriously considered quitting my job and just going home in one piece. Then I remembered, *"The **brain** is the most powerful weapon"*. I thought their brains are not functioning very well right now, (They were quite drunk.) I told myself, "I can handle this", and walked over to their table and sat down. They were shocked - one said, "Who the F___ are you?"

With a smile on my face I introduced myself. "My name is John, (I reached out and shook hands with each one), and I need to have a talk with you guys. The owner, (and I pointed to him, a small little man, standing in the corner), has asked me to throw you three out of the bar. (They started laughing.) Now you know, I can't do that; however, I am very good at what I do, and have to try or lose my job. I really need my job. If it becomes physical, I'm good enough to permanently cripple or even kill at least one, or maybe two, of you before you beat the shit out of me. Now I don't want to get beat to a pulp, and I don't think any of you need to die or get crippled tonight, so why don't the three of you just go down the street a block to the Attic, and keep on having fun, instead of going to jail, when that little fart of an owner over there, calls the police. There's no place on the island to hide, and the jail is really old, cold and uncomfortable."

One of them said, "He's making sense to me". They all got up, gave the owner the finger as they left, and were gone. The owner came over to me, and asked, what I said to them? I told him, all I said was that you were an ass hole, and I didn't want to get hurt. He didn't fire me; he gave me a raise. *The brain truly is the best weapon.*

As important as focusing is, you still need to be aware of what is going on around you. situation awareness is what we call it. It is easy to concentrate on a single situation and assume you have it under control. That assumption may get you in trouble, if you lose track of what options are actually available.

This is a story of just such a situation. During a military training session on bayonet defensive action, the trainer was a tough old time Sergeant. He had a rifle with a wooden bayonet on it. The trainees had the same thing. The drill was for the trainee to charge the trainer and get him with their bayonet.

The drill was going as expected. The trainer was deflecting the trainee's weapon and hitting them with the butt of his gun. The first five trainees were easily dispatched by the trainer. The next trainee, (who shall remain unnamed), decided he didn't want to get hit in the head by the butt of the trainer's gun. Having had the gift of watching the previous five get wacked, he remembered the brain is the best weapon. The trainer was completely focused on the attacking rifle, not on the person carrying it.

He charged the trainer, just like the others had, thrusting his rifle forward. The trainer knocked the gun aside with his gun, realizing too late that the trainee had let go of his gun, to block a right cross to his chin. The trainer went down while the trainee picked up his gun and pinned the Sergeant to the ground.

The trainer got up and said," I'll be dammed, that will never happen again." He shook the trainee's hand and thanked him for the lesson. The drill went on and he was right, it never happened again. Never lose, *situation awareness,* walking home at night, driving your car, or just eating dinner. Always be aware of what is going on around you, and who is watching.

5

Teaching School

When I was five or six years old, I met a man that showed me what good teaching was all about. I never forgot him, or what he taught me about how to teach. I wrote about him In Vol. I of Life…. *"The Fish"*, is the story. Growing up I knew I wanted to be a teacher, but thought it would never happen; you had to go to college and I didn't plan to do that. The only thing in life that is certain is change. I was extremely fortunate that one of the changes in my life sent me to college and I could fulfill my dream. I became a teacher.

I retired from teaching when I was 57 years old, due to a loss of hearing that was impairing my ability to answer questions in the class room. The one thing that I never wanted to happen was to become an incompetent teacher. It was time for me to retire.

I taught high school for two years and college for 28 years, and always tried to teach like Dr. Carl Hubs taught me to identify a fish in 1941. *Never tell them what they want to know, guide them so they can **discover** it themselves.* It is the best teaching philosophy I know of, and Hubs taught it to me in just 20 minutes.

I had one more person that shaped the way I should, and did, treat every one of my students. He said, *I had to love each one of them like they were one of my own children.* I didn't have to like them, but I did need to love them. They had to earn my respect, but no matter what, *I had to love them so I would* **never give up on them.** He told me, they may not like you, but they will still learn from you if they feel you really care for them, much like their real parents. His name was John Wozny, my master teacher at Huntington Beach High School, when I was a student teacher in training.

I credit those two men with 90% of any success I had in my teaching career. I told every class I taught the first day, "When you walk through the door into my class room, you are one of my kids for the rest of your life". Most of them just laughed and forgot it, but I meant it. I have had several dozen past students over the years call me on the phone and ask my advice, about some problem, I guess they believed me.

I loved teaching. I taught at several of our local junior colleges, two high schools, and six universities; I told the students in all my classes not to call me professor, just refer to me as teacher or coach. I communicated to them that I was not there to profess, I was there to teach them about, and guide them into exciting and new areas of their future lives.

Like every teacher that reaches retirement, I have an unending number of stories, (I told a dozen of the funniest ones in Vol. I). I have just two, very special ones I will share with you here. They both show what can be accomplished when the above teaching philosophy is followed.

I taught many different subjects during my 28 years at Santa Ana College – among them was Archery. I also taught classes in the physically challenged department (PCD). They held special classes for these special people. I taught self-defense, which required special skills depending on the student's impairment, and in the circuit training room physical exercise classes, that also required special programs for each student.

The head of the PCD asked if I would teach an archery class for their department. I told her I would be honored to do that. All of the classes I had taught for her department had been a challenge for me, I loved that, and I met some wonderfully inspiring people.

The new semester started and I was on my way to meet my archery class for the first time. I had the roll sheet in my hand, with five names on it. The small number in the class was standard for these classes, so the teacher had time to work with each one on an individual basis.

When I arrived on the field, they were all there and seemed excited. I had brought a bow and some arrows to demonstrate how to string the bow and handle the equipment. I immediately discovered, my plan A, wasn't going to work, and I did not have a plan B to move to at that moment. (It would come later.)

I had five very different individuals. One in a wheel chair, that was a paraplegic. He would be fine and could shoot from his chair. I recognized him from a judo class a few years before, and asked him why he was in the chair. He was the victim of a drive by shooting, (How suddenly our lives can change).

One of the others was also in a wheel chair. He had no use of his left arm. He could not speak, and had a small typing machine strapped to his left arm. He typed on it with his right hand, which produced a small tape out of the machine. It was his only way to communicate. He had a helper that pushed the chair for him.

There was a girl with a wheel chair who was standing behind it. She informed me that her medication was in the bag on the back of her chair and, if she fell down, to get the pills in the red bottle and give her one, or if her tremors got too bad, (they were intermittent), to give her one of the pills in the green bottle. What would my administration say about that? I didn't want to know, so I didn't ask.

There was a man with a cane. He was going to be to be ok, I thought, until he told me he could not stand up, without the cane.

The last one was going to be the biggest challenge, she was blind – not just a little bit - totally blind.

I talked to all of them, taking notes on each one; *I promised I would work out a plan for each of them*, by the time we met next week. The boy, with the tape machine, handed me a tape as we were leaving that said, "How can I shoot?" I didn't know what to say; I had no idea, I just told him, "Let me work on it".

I walked into the physical education office, sat down in a chair, and just sat there. The secretary asked me, "Are you alright?"

I answered her, "I just came from my archery class, and for the first time in my 15 years of teaching, I going to find out what kind of a teacher I really am". I told her about the class.

She asked, "What are you going to do?"

Shaking my head, I said, "I don't know right now, but I have five days to figure something out." It was Thursday; the class met again the next Tuesday. I went home, sat down with my notes, took one at a time, to figure all of my options specifically for each individual. I remembered the words from my master teacher, **"So you will never give up on them"**.

I am going to set the stage to help you understand my solutions. In a normal archery class the targets are set up in a line, being sure there is nothing behind them that could be hurt by a stray arrow. The archers stand in a line in front of the targets at various distances, but all at the same distance at the same time, and all shoot at the same time. Then they all go to their target and retrieve their arrows, at the same time. I realized that would not work with these students. Some would shoot fairly fast, others were going to be very slow. Some will shoot at 30 yards, and some at ten feet.

I went to my dean on Friday, and told him about the class, and that I had to have the entire track and the football field area, totally closed off during my class time. He agreed to make that happen. I ended up having the archers stand in a small circle, in the middle of the football field, back to back, split up so they were shooting in three different groups, in different directions, each group at its own speed, and distance. This allowed me to work with each one, without holding up the others from shooting. I did not want any of them to get bored having to wait to shoot for a long time.

By the next meeting I had worked out a way for each of them to shoot. I didn't have a choice, *I had made a promise to them.*

The first one was easy. He was confined to the chair, but was fine in the upper body. He could use a regular bow and handle it just fine.

The second one, with no use of his left arm, needed something designed special for him. I remembered reading about a bow pistol. It was a crossbow, but in miniature, to become a pistol. It was not a toy. I found one in an archery shop and bought it. My student had a full-time helper to push him in his chair, and he could load the bow for him, so he could shoot holding the pistol grip in his right hand. He was ecstatic.

My girl with the tremors never had any trouble that I had to get the meds out of the bag on the chair for, but she did have trouble knowing when to release the arrows. She would be aiming the bow at full draw, and have a tremor, releasing the arrow. Many of her arrows ended up in very strange places, like the one that went clear over the fence around the field, 60 yards away, onto the main street full of moving cars. We didn't hear any crashes, but we didn't go looking for that arrow, either.

The man with the cane that couldn't stand up wasn't a problem. I just had a chair for him each class to sit in and shoot from.

The blind girl was a different kind of problem. She was physically in good shape, she just could not see. I had asked her if she got around a lot from the sounds in her environment. She said she did. I bought a metronome, and brought it to the class, set it up ten feet from her, and she pointed right to it. I set the tic toc machine on top of the archery target, only ten feet out, and she could hit the target throwing a ball, every time, even if I turned her around. She would turn back and hit the target. I figured if I taught her the proper stance, and she became consistent with it, she could shoot.

She learned how to stand and hold the bow, exactly the same way every time. She listened, and took a stance at the sound. I had her shoot an arrow. She, of course, couldn't know where it hit the target. I would tell her where it did. She would then change her stance to compensate, and bring the next arrow closer to the center of the target. If the arrow has high, the back foot was moved forward towards the target. If the arrow was to the left, she moved her backfoot to the left. After adjusting the first two arrows, she could shoot a nice group of the next four arrows right in or near the center. We started at ten feet, and by the end of the class she was shooting at 15 yards She was incredible.

The mother of the young man that only had use of one hand and couldn't speak, came to the school at the end of the class, and talked to my dean. She wanted him to know that her son loved the class and wanted to thank me, and the school, for taking the time to work with him. She said I made a difference in his life. It seems no one else had ever paid any attention to him. When my dean called me into his office, and told me what she said, I teared up. She had no way of knowing, *he was one of my kids too.*

Retirement

After I retired, I moved to the state of Washington. One morning, after living there for three years, I got a phone call. I was asked if I would teach a marine biology class for Peninsula College. It was located in Port Angeles, 40 miles away, but had a field station in Port Townsend. I lived in Port Ludlow, only 13 miles from the class location. The person who was scheduled to teach the class had to back out at the last minute and they needed a teacher. Someone told someone that told someone that I was a retired marine biology teacher, and I got a call. It was the dean for the schools' outstation classes.

She interviewed me and offered me the job. I accepted. She said, "You didn't ask how much it paid?"

I told her it didn't make any difference, I was not doing it for the money, but rather for the opportunity to be with my kids again, I missed them. The class was just once a year, for 12 weeks. It was not going to interrupt my retirement. It was held at the end of the pier, in an aquarium building. The room was small, only room for 25 students, perfect for a hard of hearing teacher to still be competent. I loved being in the classroom again and taught the class for six years.

It was during this time that I met a very special young man. I was explaining the class procedures during the first class meeting. I told them that I gave a quiz the first thing every class meeting. It was on the reading assignment that I gave for home work, the preceding class. After class this young man came to me and told me, he was going to have to drop the class. I asked him why?

He told me he was bipolar, and had spent most of his life heavily sedated, and could not write. He had not finished high school because he couldn't pass the tests. He could not write them out. I asked him why he signed up for this class. He said he wanted an education and wanted to try a class to see if he could do it now that he was older. (He had been out of school for a few years). He said he now realized that it would be impossible for him. I had to think fast, his dad came to pick him up, and they were starting to walk down the pier to leave. I called to them, "Wait a minute, I have an idea". They came back.

I told them about auditing the class. He could attend the entire class and not have to take any test. He would not get credit for it, but he could enjoy and learn just the same. He said he would love to do that. I told him that by a certain date, a few weeks off, he would have to be sure to switch to an audit from a regular student, so it would not show up as a failure.

When the time came for him to switch, he came to me and asked if he could stay as a regular student. He said he was understanding the class material and really wanted to try. He had been very active in all of our discussions in class, and was obviously reading all the assignments. He had missed the first four quizzes; I told him that I would give him an oral test on that material, so he would not lose those points towards his grade. He knew the material better than most of the other students. I gave him oral tests the rest of the class, including the final. *He earned a B.* He and his father, were overjoyed. He said, "Maybe I can get an education after all". I lost contact with him right after that.

Years later I was at our local movie theater with my wife and some friends. When the movie was over, the lights came on and we all stood up to leave, he and his family were sitting right in front of us. He turned around, put his arms around me and said, "You don't know what you did for me. *"You taught me I could"*. His mother hugged me and started to cry, of course I did too. His father was crying, my wife started to cry. We were standing in the middle of all the people that were trying to leave the theater crying, and the movie was a comedy. It turns out, that he had gone to school, requested oral exams until he could write them, and was in the final semester to become a nurse. There are lots of good teachers out there.

Teaching was my calling. When my mother had said that I was born ready, I just needed to find out what for. She was right. I was lucky, I found out. Teaching was truly my first love when it came to working. Now in my 80s, writing is my work, and I love it, too. Being a writer enables me to still be a teacher. My life of wonder just keeps expanding.

We are all students our entire life, because there is so much to learn, however, we are also all teachers, because we are the ones that others around us, will learn from. Set a good example, Be a good teacher.

Teachers come in many different shapes and forms, depending on what and where they are teaching. Even the same person can change and have many identities, life is so much fun.

6

Bike Riding/Racing

When I was going to college at Long Beach State College, (now Cal State University at Long Beach), I decided to ride a bike to school. It was 20 miles, and my part-time job was in Seal Beach at Dow Chemical Company on the way to the college. It would save me money, and keep me in shape. It was a win-win situation. I could then leave the car with my wife and my newborn son, so we only needed one car.

COSTA MESA CYCLIST JOHN RESECK II
Pedal Pusher Takes Son John III for Ride

It was working out well, and I was getting in good bicycle riding shape. I rode 16 miles to work, four miles to school after work, and then 20 miles home, every day. All but a couple of miles of my trip was on the Coast Highway between Long Beach and Newport, a straight and flat road along the beach. Many bikers used it as part of their training rides. They would pass me with their heads down, riding in tight groups. One day I decided to tag along with a group of five as they whizzed by, to see if I could keep up with them. I did for about five miles, then they pulled away from me.

The group rode at the same time every Tuesday, and Thursday, and I was going home at that time. I decided to chase them every time they came by me. After a month, they couldn't shake me off so they stopped, and talked to me. Who was I, why was I riding there on a schedule, was I training to race? I told them I was just coming home from school. They said I should be racing on weekends with their club. They were from the Orange County Wheelmen Club.

The idea of racing had never entered my mind. I didn't even know there were bike races. Being a competitor at heart, I had to try it, I wasn't competing in anything else at that particular time.

I found out very quickly that my rides to school and back didn't cut it for racing training. I changed my route home to 55 miles, instead of the 20 I had been doing; and now I had my head down, too. After another month they told me I was ready to ride in my first race as a novice.

I was excited and had no idea how I would do in a real competition. There were about 15 riders in the novice class ready to give it their all, and I was one of them. As I remember you had to place 1st or 2nd, in a novice race to to proceed to a class C rider.

The race started and was 25 miles. We were all together for the first 15 miles, then there was a steep hill about a quarter of a mile long. One of the young whipper snappers took off up the hill like a madman. We all stood up on our bikes to catch him. I was catching him slowly, and I was only 50 feet behind him, the top of the hill was very close now so I sat back down on my seat and figured I would make up the 50 feet on the downhill. WOW! What a mistake that was. He was right in front of me when he went over the top, but when I got to the top of the hill, just seconds later, he had 50 yards on me and disappearing down the hill. In the few miles to the finish I gained back a lot but I never caught him. I learned a very valuable lesson that day. Don't ever give an inch, even if you think you are doing good at whatever it is you are doing. I have two short stories, where I taught some other riders this lesson.

We raced every weekend somewhere in the area. This race was a short one of 30 miles, and was in Orange County, ending up by going through Santiago Canyon and finishing at a restaurant called Cooks Corner. It was near my house and I rode the route during my training rides, as did some of my biking friends.

Near the end of this race was a hill we all hated. It was steep and about a third of a mile long, with a sharp turn near the top that broke the pedaling rhythm of the rider on the climb to make the turn. It was like starting from a dead stop, right in the steepest part of the climb, but we could see the top ahead, which gave us the motivation to get over it.

There were about 20 riders in the race, and because it was short, we were not able to leave anyone behind yet when we hit the bottom of our hill. On the way up, to the turn, the riders all strung out with only ten riders reaching the turn as a group, including myself and three of my local friends.

Rounding the turn and starting on the steepest part of the hill, we were all hurting. One of the riders shouted, "How much farther is it to the top of this SOB?"

I shouted back to him, so everyone could hear, "Don't worry, we're almost half way". The four locals kept the pedal rate up, the rest of them folded, and dropped back. The picture below tells the rest of the story. We placed, one, two, three and four, of course, I was third.

One type of race was called a Criterion. This one was again local so I entered it even though I hadn't raced for almost a year; as far as bike racing was concerned, I was an old man. This was a fun race and I would see some of my friends there. It was a 25-mile race, broken into five parts. We rode a five-mile circular course, getting points each time we crossed the start line for the first five places. Points were added up at the end of the race to determine what riders would get the trophies. I was tied with an 18-year-old for fourth place.

The judges told the two of us to go back a quarter of a mile and start our own race, to see who would get the fourth-place trophy. The boy's father had ridden in the Olympics sometime in the past and was there to watch his son race. The boy was riding a single gear sprint bike and I had a 10-speed road bike. Everyone knew the boy was going to win. His bike was built for this type of race. We started ourselves, riding slowly watching each other.

I knew that if we got near the finish line, before we took off, I was dead meat. I had thought about it and decided if I could get him to jump early, I might be able to catch him. I stood up on the bike and he reacted liked I thought he would, and took off leaving me in the dust, but way too soon. He jumped a good 100 feet out in front but reached his top speed about the same time. I was winding up through my gears and finally caught him but was too tired to keep up that pace.

I looked over at him and said, "Give up kid, you just don't have it". He just sat down and quit. He could have beaten me, and should have, but didn't. His father ran up to him and asked him what happened. He told his dad, "I just didn't have it". His dad came over to me and said that was a lesson his son needed to learn, and this was the best place for him to learn it, when it wasn't important.

I raced a few years and found out there was always someone just a little better than me. I took a lot of Second and Third place trophies, but very few First-place ones. I was always there at the finish but the sprinters beat me every time. It wasn't until much later that I learned about red and white muscle fibers. At least I finally figured out why I was such a bad sprinter – not enough white fibers. The red ones give you endurance and I had lots of those; the white ones give you fast muscle contraction for the sprint and I was lacking in those.

My cycling became a 55-mile ride, three days a week, with a friend. Together, over a period of 15 years, we rode 13,000 miles. We rode the bike trail through Huntington Beach most of the time, at a soft 15 miles an hour. We saw many of the same people that used the trail on a regular basis like we did.

One of the regulars was a young woman that had a small child on the rear of her bike in a child bike chair. The baby always had a helmet on, but the mother didn't. One morning I said to her as she passed us, (she was a hot rider,) "It's a good thing the baby has a helmet on". She answered back, "I don't want a child with a scrambled brain". I called to her as she rode on, "He doesn't want a mama with one either".

The next time we saw them, they both had helmets on. It used to amaze me, when I was patrolling the docks in the harbors for the Coast Guard, how many families would be strolling along the docks looking at the boats, with a couple of very young kids, with no lifejackets on, but their dog, was wearing one. Sometimes we just don't think.

Biking/racing taught me I was capable of pushing beyond what I thought was my best. It also made me realize I had to think I could, before I could, and that applied to everything. To say, *I can't do something is a self-fulfilling prophecy. It's the mind that controls the body, and the mind is always listening,* even if you don't say it out loud and it won't let you lie.

7

Antarctic Expedition

1958

When I graduated with my Bachler's degree, I realized I still had more questions than answers, about everything. I wanted to be a teacher that had a wide range of information, so that I could put the sciences I loved and was teaching into an everyday perspective to help the student understand why they needed to know it

I talked to the University of Washington and the University of California Irvine about a PhD program. One wanted me to work on plankton, the other a single family of fish for my projects. I could not see where working for three years to narrow my knowledge was going to help me be the kind of teacher I envisioned myself to be.

I took a semester off and went to work for my uncle, Mel; he built pottery kilns. I was just a roustabout but learned to be a brick layer while there. When it came time to start the next semester, I had the money to go back to school and had decided to get a Masters in Biology, with an emphasis in the marine environment. They did not offer a Marine Biology program at that time at Long Beach State.

It was while I was working on the Biology Degree that my master advisor, R.G. Miller, received a grant to go to the Antarctic and work on fish. He asked me to be his assistant on the expedition – it was part of the "International Geophysical Year, (IGY)". I became a member of a six-man unit being sent to McMurdo Station, Antarctic, to study the biology of the area. It was the first such unit ever sent by the USA to the Antarctic. The expedition was called," Operation Deepfreeze". It was 1958.

I knew nothing about Antarctica except where it was and that it was the only place on earth that was considered a continent and was not yet explored. For me, it was like walking on the moon. I did some research and found out all I could in the time available to me. I was being sent to McMurdo Station, in the Ross Sea, to study fish.

The first boat to reach the edge of the pack ice in front of the Ross Sea was from Australia, the 'Venus', in 1831. Some of our history books go back thousands of years. The history books on the Ross Sea are less than 200 years old. The Ross Sea, (RS), itself was not discovered until 1840, when Captain Ross was the first to break through the pack ice into the sea that now bears his name. The fish of the RS were not collected until 1900 when the British expedition, "Southern Cross", looked at the ichthyofauna for the first time and described seven new species of fish.

ONE OF OUR CHOPPERS PICKING UP SUPPLIES TO MOVE TO ANOTHER STATION.

The famous Scott expedition, *Discovery,* (1901-1904), also collected fish and added three more species to the list of fish found in the RS. By the time I was going to the RS to collect fish, (1958), there were a fairly large number of other fishes on the list that were also found in other regions of the Antarctica inshore waters.

To make a point of just how **recent this important history is**, in 1958-1959, when our unit of scientists were deployed on the ice, we can look at what was happening in the world during those two years.

In 1958 – Sir Edmond Hillary, the first man to top Mount Everest also visited the South Pole on a New Zealand expedition – Michael Jackson was born – Tyrone Power died – the big books/movies were *Dr. Zhivago, Breakfast at Tiffany's and Gigi* – the big songs were, Catch A Falling Star and *The Purple People Eater.*

In 1959 – American Air Lines started the first coast to coast jet air service – the Belgian Antarctic expedition took along *20 hula hoops* – the US Postal service bands, *Lady Chatterley's Lover,* from the US Mail – the first telephone cable connecting the USA to Europe is completed – 12 nations sign a treaty that the Antarctic shall be a war free zone, and open to all countries for scientific research – big songs were, *He's Got The Whole World In His Hands, Tom Dooley, Everything Is Coming Up Roses* and *Mack The Knife*.

In researching for this story, I came across something that made me proud, but very surprised. The book was, *The History of Antarctic Fishes*. The passage that caught my attention, quote, "In this, Mr. John Reseck Jr., a graduate student representing Long Beach, was assiduous and highly successful in obtaining a representative series of Ross Sea fishes." I thought that can't be me, this is a *history book*. Then I looked in the mirror, and decided that it really was me.

Dr. Miller and I were not the only ones there to study the bio-fauna of the area. There were six of us, all working within our biological specialties. We were told at the station, that our group of six was the first team of scientists to be sent by the United States to specifically study the biology of the ice covered continent. Most of the research being done at that time was geo-physical.

Our unit consisted of two from Stanford, Dr. Wohlschlag, (cold water fish physiology) and John Dearborn, (marine Invertebrates) – two from Long Beach, Dr. Miller and myself, (both fish taxonomy) – one from Oak ridge, Matt Pryor, (his project was not known to me), and one from a college on the East Coast, Dr. Worthy, (land plants-moss and lichens). We all had individual projects and helped each other whenever we could.

DR. WOHLSCHLAG & DR. DEWITT

DR. PRYOR & DR. DELL-NEW ZEALAND

Dr. Miller traveled to Hallett Station soon after we got to the ice and was unable to return to McMurdo for the entire summer, due to the ice at Hallett Station becoming too thin for a plane to land on. I took over his duties at McMurdo, including representing the USA on the New Zealand oceanographic cruise aboard the HMS Endeavour, under the control of Dr. Dell. Dr. Miller continued his project with the fish he collected through the ice, at Hallett Station.

McMurdo Station was a combination of plywood structures – canvas tent-like structures called James-way and even one that was a huge dome inflated with air from a compressor that never shut off. The station was located on the back edge of the Ross Ice Shelf, on land. We slept, 8 to 12 men, in each James-way.

There were Navy, CBs, Air force, and Army personnel and us (they called us IGYS, International Geophysical Year Scientist), for a total of (as close as I can remember), 125+/- people.

The CBs were working on building a permanent station at McMurdo. While I was there, they were working hard to scrape the perma-frost out so roads could be created. The big D-8 Caterpillars they were using, could only scrap off about one half of an inch of perma-frost at a time. A very slow process.

The Navy was in charge of the station and the air contingency was, I believe, all Navy pilots as well. Everyone was mixed together in the same cold-weather gear and I couldn't tell one from another. My inability to recognize military rank got me in trouble.

I was in the mess hall for dinner and when I left, I took the wrong cap. We all wore the same caps; the only difference was the little emblem that was attached over the bill of the cap. I was back in my James-way getting ready to go to bed when a couple of MPs came and arrested me for impersonating an officer – a real high-ranking officer – a general. I was forgiven because I was an IGY, and didn't know any better. The whole camp had a laugh at the dumb kid that didn't recognize a General's insignia.

The IGYs were all scientists and worked, with help from the Navy, on their various projects. Between the two dog sleds, a couple of weasels and snow cats and the two helicopters, we were fairly mobile and took samples from a large area.

DEARBORN, PULLING TRAPS

Some of our equipment was quite primitive. A good example was the two-inch ice chisel we used to cut holes in the ice. The ice was five feet thick where we were. We cut holes that were three by four feet, to drop our specimen collecting traps through. I caught fish in them and Dearborn caught invertebrates in them. It took us two or three days to chip through five feet of ice with a two-inch chisel welded onto a six-foot steel one-inch in diameter shaft. We tried blasting a hole through with a 40-pound shape charge. It worked, but the hole was only one foot in diameter and of little use to us.

When the big vehicles like the D-8 Cats, and snow-cats were traveling over the glacier-covered land, they had long arms protruding out in front of them with sonar crevasse detectors on the ends to keep them from breaking through the ice bridges and dropping into a crevasse. Even with that equipment, they still lost one Cat coming back from Little America station, to McMurdo station, when they were in the process of closing down the Little America station.

CLEARING ICE FROM THE HOLE

The cold weather caused many small problems that were expected, such as frostbite, and frozen fuel for the vehicles. The warmest day we had during my four months stay was 32 degrees, and the coldest day was only 60 degrees below zero. It was summer.

Every once in a while, we had a white-out condition. That is when the wind blows so hard that it moves the small ice chips, and snow on the surface; it is like being in a heavy snow storm. You can't see anything. If you are caught out on the ice you have to honker down and not try to move anywhere. You can't see the cracks in the ice, or tell what direction you are going. All vehicles have to stop in place, but they can't turn their engines off; if they do the fuel freezes and they cannot restart it to get back to the station. If an air plane is in the air they can't land because they have no way to tell where the landing surface is.

In a totally frozen environment where it is impossible to dig a hole, what do you do with human waste? There are no flush toilets and you can't dig a hole for an outhouse in permafrost – what are 125 men going to do about that? Their answer, I thought, was ingenious. They built a raised platform with six outhouses on it, and put an empty 50-gallon drum under each hole. There was no smell because it froze instantly in the barrel. When the barrels were full, they were taken to the edge of the ice shelf miles away to fall into the ocean, when the ice melted.

Where do you find water in a frozen environment? Not hard to figure out. Ice was melted as our fresh water supply. To convert the ice into water, however, fuel had to be used to create the heat, and fuel was in a limited supply – it was needed to run all of the vehicles and heat the living quarters. That created a rationing of our water; we could only have one short shower a week. Since my time there, McMurdo station has been enlarged a little at a time and is now a small city.

The IGY scientists all completed their projects, publishing many papers and were the pioneers for an ongoing United States Antarctic Research Program, USARP. The IGY personnel created the foundation for the exploration of the Antarctic by the United States explores that came after them.

It was a dangerous place in the late 1950s. We had eight or ten of the military personnel killed, due to accidents, during my stay. There was a plane crash that killed all aboard, just doing routine work in good weather. One of the D-8 Cats fell through an ice bridge into a crevasse and fell some 100 feet before it was stopped by the crevasse getting to narrow too pass. The men in its cab survived with one of them breaking his arm.

The word of the accident was radioed to McMurdo Station and a helicopter was sent to pick up the injured man. There were several people at the station that were representing magazines and newspapers and were looking for stories to write. One of them got really excited that he was going to be able to record the injured man's first words as he got out of the chopper, and he would have an exclusive for his radio station back home.

The helicopter landed and he was there with his head phones and recorder, all checked out to be sure there would be no problem with this once in a lifetime chance for him to get something no one else had. The medics took a stretcher into the chopper and were carrying the injured man out on it. The reporter rushed up and stuck his microphone out to the man and asked," What happened out there?" The answer wasn't what he was expecting.

"I fell into a crevasse, you stupid asshole, and broke my F------ arm. Now get out of the way so these guys can fix it," The newsman, stunned, stepped back out of the way, and just stared as they carried the stretcher off. All of us standing around were hysterical. So much for his moment of fame. One of the injured man's CB buddies was there, and said, "That news guy thought he was in Central Park; this is the end of the earth and that was a CB he was talking to, what the hell did he expect?"

I would guess that it is still dangerous because there are many edges to walk on in the Antarctic, and the researchers always push the envelope, that is just what we do. The saying, *"If you're not walking on the edge of life, you're taking up too much room." is the motto of all wonderers.* I accept that, however, I now use a walking stick, so I won't fall off.

**JOHN RESECK JR,
A WONDERER IN ONE OF HIS CLASS ROOMS**

The question is what did this expedition teach me? I was 23 years old, raised on a farm and the intercity, had never traveled anywhere or been around the military – I was like a five-year-old – everything around me was new. I can't even imagine all the things I learned about science, about expedition life, about the military, about the difference between need and want, and about life in the real world. When my mother found out I was going on the expedition, she told my aunt, "It will be a good thing for Johnny. He'll get all the travel out of his system." It's the only time I can ever remember her being wrong. I have not stopped traveling since the day I came home from the ice. Now in my 80s, I still travel at least one week every month, somewhere.

What did I learn? The highlights would have to be – that I could hold my own with some of the best scientist the US and New Zealand had to offer – that the difference between need and want is as big as the Grand Canyon – That no matter where you live, you are on the edge of life all the time (situation awareness) – How important the people around you are, (choose your friends as if your life depends on them, because it might) – no matter what you plan, make a, *what If list*, at least mentally, so you always have a plan B ready – and finally, CBs are really tough dudes, and make great friends..

8

The Coast Guard Auxiliary

When I retired from Santa Ana College, I moved to Port Ludlow, Washington. I had my C-Dory with me on a boat trailer, with the intention of doing a lot of fishing. Port Ludlow is a small town built around a beautiful harbor and has everything you would expect in a mostly retirement community. It has a golf course, hundreds of boats, a fine hotel, a yacht club, a good restaurant and, of course, a Coast Guard Auxiliary flotilla to keep us all safe boaters.

Retirement is a major time/change in your life. I now define it as, *"The only time in your life when you have the time to become totally over committed"*. I did not realize, until I was totally over-committed, that I was. I joined the golf clubs both 9 and 18 holes, the yacht club, the local potluck fellowship group and the fly-fishing club. I also started a kayaking club. I struggled along for two years trying to keep up/active in all of it; I was falling behind in everything. That is just not who I am, I was getting depressed. I asked myself, what is your first love? It was a simple answer, the ocean all around us; it was why we moved there

I decided to stay active and concentrate on the kayak club, along with joining the Coast Guard Auxiliary. I dropped all of the others. All of my activity now was on the water or in a class room teaching boating to new boaters. I was a happy camper once again. My wife, Sharon, joined the CGAux. with me. I spent my time on the water, doing patrols and teaching boating classes; she became the major computer person entering all the CG data for our entire division. We both loved our jobs and retired from the Coast Guard Auxiliary after 18 years, when we moved back to California.

While Sharon became the expert, on the Olympic Peninsula, with the Coast Guard data program. I became a Qualifying Examiner, (QE). I trained and tested members so they could receive the qualifications to be part of the crew on our Coast Guard boats during official Patrols.

Most of my time on patrols was spent cruising the Puget Sound waters waiting for the Coast Guard to call, requesting us to render aid to some boater with a problem. That was boring, but the Coast Guard also used us, and our boats, to be the bad guys during some of their training exercises. They were both exciting and, sometimes, more fun than I can describe. There were a couple of our exercises that I will never forget, and will enjoy sharing with you.

The exercises were mostly part of the war games the military uses to train the new recruits. Our Flotilla was near the nuclear sub base in the Hood Canal. It was a highly guarded area by patrol boats; no one was allowed get close to the subs. The Navy had a new patrol boat they wanted to try out and train the crew on. They called on us, the Coast Guard Aux., and our boats to be the bad guys and try to get our boats into the restricted area through their patrol boats. They did not know which of the many boats that passed the base would be ours. We just acted like any other boat passing by. Then we would make a sharp turn, head for the protected area going as fast as our boat could go, to get in before they could catch us.

Their boats were faster than most of ours so we would try to get away by cutting back and forth through the water. They chased us shooting very loud blanks out of a 50-caliber machine gun, mounted on the bow of their boat. When we thought they got us we set off a smoke flare on our boat to show them we had been hit. You can imagine what this would look like to someone that didn't know what was going on right off a nuclear submarine base.

We were doing all this about one mile south of the mile-long Hood Canal Bridge. The cars driving over the bridge had a bird's eye view of the whole thing. There was a flood of 911 calls to the police, who knew nothing about the exercise, from the cars that were now stopped on the bridge, clogging traffic, as well as the home owners who lived along the shore of the canal, who were worried about a terrorist attack on the sub base. I am quite sure the Navy never had another exercise like that one without telling the local authorities, ahead of time. They had a lot of explaining to do.

The next story involves a situation where the exercise was to protect a convoy of many ships. There are procedures the Navy has to best protect the convoy when the ships are attacked, and we were going to practice one of them.

Our auxiliary boats, (10 of them), formed into a long single line 75 yards apart, with a Navy patrol boat alongside it in front, and one on the other side of it towards the back. The CGAux. boats were the convoy. Each of the convoy boats (our boats were yachts of various shapes and sizes), was carrying a Navy officer on it that had a diversion plan for the particular type of ship we were representing in the convoy (tanker, troop ship, etc.) to execute when we were attacked.

We were told we would be attacked at some time during the prescribed course by a high-speed boat that would try to get in position to sink us with torpedoes. When it attacked the convoy would scatter, according to plan, and the Navy patrol boats would chase the bad guys down and sink them. Everyone involved had guns shooting blanks, but making a lot of noise and smoke.

These exercises were a lot of fun for us, but also were very important. They allowed the Navy to see if they had a plan that would work in a real situation. Everyone took them very seriously and played their part to the best of their ability to make it as real as possible.

The convoy was formed up and moving through the straits of Juan De Fuca at a speed of eight knots, about 10 mph, when a yacht that was just crossing the straits saw us, going the same direction as he was, and just pulled into our line at the rear. I was on the last convoy boat and he pulled in behind us. I went to the radio to tell him to drop off, but he was not monitoring the radio like he should have been. Before I could take any other action - we were attacked.

The attack boat came around from behind an island doing 50+ knots, with its guns blazing. The convoy boats all jumped to flank (top) speed and turned in all directions as to their specific instructions. The patrol boats, of course, with guns firing 50 caliber blanks that are really loud, took chase.

The attack boat, coming from the rear, passed between the boat I was on and the yacht behind us, with a Navy boat in hot pursuit both with guns blazing. There was no question, it was a war zone. The man on the fly bridge at the helm of the yacht hit the deck with his hands covering his head. His boat, with no one at the wheel, went into a tight circle.

There were boats going in every direction, and gunfire coming from most of them. After about five minutes the word came over the radio that the exercise was over, and it was quiet again. By now, word had been passed to the patrol boats about the yacht in the rear not being part of the exercise. One of the patrol boats went to the yacht and told them, over a loud speaker, to leave the area - they were in the middle of a Navy training exercise. The yacht left at flank speed. I think the skipper had to hurry home and change his underwear.

This is another training exercise but quite different. The troops involved were from all branches of the services, and there were about 1200 of them living in tents on an island, one-half mile off shore. It was a Navy base. The CG Aux. was asked to see if we could infiltrate the camp at night and do some kind of damage, (not real damage, of course). This was the kind of training I had years ago when I was called a "Spook". I saw it as a chance to relive my youth and volunteered to be the one to try.

I had to have one of the military people from the camp with me, to make sure that I played by the rules and didn't get into any real trouble. They sent me a corpsman from the hospital; he was an old timer. When he showed up at midnight to meet me, he had made some packages that said, "bomb", on them for us to plant if we were not caught in time to prevent us from planting them. He was as excited about the mission as I was.

I knew the island had radar and heat sensors to detect anyone as they approached the island from the water. They would be expecting us to be coming from the land side of the camp. The island was connected to the mainland on the back side. I chose to come from the water side directly into the camp, where they figured they had it covered.

I had a Kevlar two-man kayak and a graphite paddle, neither of which would show well on radar. The kayak was only 28 inches wide and, low in the water coming towards the shore would look like surface scatter in a choppy sea. The heat sensors were a different problem. The year before, when the same exercise was tried, the heat sensors spotted the invaders on the way to the beach. When they landed on the beach there was a group of cadets there to capture them the minute they stepped ashore. I didn't want that to happen to us.

I had my partner hold a large golf umbrella, that had been dipped in the water, in front of us so we would not be picked up as a hot spot on the thermal sensors. It worked, we paddled up to the shore, pulled our boat to the bottom of the eight-foot cliff that ran along the beach, and were not detected.

Crawling on our bellies in the long shadows of some trees, we made it into the camp proper. There were at least a hundred tents in the camp, but my partner, being from the camp, knew which tent the Captain in charge of the entire program slept in.

I crawled to his tent and hung one of our flags, (We had created a flag to represent our fictious country during the war exercises.), over the front of his tent. That was the same thing as saying, "you are dead!" Then we planted some of our "bombs" in the motor pool as we crawled on our bellies under the trucks.

On our way to the radar station we had to pass the field hospital. That was where my partner worked. He was a Corpsman. He had me wait while he went in and killed all the personal on duty in the hospital, then we preceded to the radar station.

At the radar station there was a guard standing outside, looking out at the ocean. We snuck up behind him and when he turned around said, "Bang your dead. Sit down and shut up". He did. Then we entered the mobile station, (it was a trailer), and killed every one there, except one. We told him to call in to headquarters and report they were under fire and had dead and wounded. That created a new and unexpected problem for them to solve. No one responded from the medical center – they had all been killed.

A detachment was sent to capture us, which wasn't too hard. We were waiting for them to get us; our mission was over. They arrived and took us into custody, putting plastic handcuffs around our wrists, behind our backs. They wanted to know how we got there? I told them in a kayak. The young man asking the questions, looked at me and asked, "How old are you?", I told him I was part of the Coast Guard underground and I was 70. He just shook his head and said," Oh shit", and walked away.

My partner was taken for questioning and I was put in a tent, with a guard outside. They had patted me down, but had missed the knife I had in the middle of my back under my belt. With my hands tied behind my back, I had access to the knife and cut my plastic cuffs off. The tent didn't have a floor so I crawled out under the side of it and walked out to the road. I flagged a jeep down and asked to be taken to the mess tent, so I could get a cup of coffee. It was 3am and a reasonable request. My kayak was at the base of the cliff right behind the mess tent. I went over the cliff, carried my boat to the water and paddled out into the dark night back to my home base.

This is why the military has training exercises. We were working with new recruits and they had to realize they could be killed if they were not at their best every moment they were on duty. There were a number of mistakes made that night that will not be made again.

The highlight for me occurred the next morning when the Captain in charge (the one I killed) came to our station and asked, who was the 70-year-old kayaker that killed him. I raised my hand, and said, *"I'm sorry"*. He presented me with a photo that he signed. It is now on my wall as the most cherished award I have ever received.

THE COAST GUARD ICE-BREAKER NORTH WIND, CLEARING A PATH THROUGH THE SEA ICE, IN THE ROSS SEA, FOR OUR SUPPLY SHIP TO MCMURDO STATION, IN THE ANTARCTICA, 1958.

Being a part of team Coast Guard, for 18 years was a time I will never forget. It was fun, worthwhile and educational, both for me and the boaters that I taught in the boating classes. It was a win-win situation. Life just can't get any better than that.

THE COAST GUARD IN ALASKA DURING AN EXERCISE, HAVING A DEBRIEFING. WHAT WENT RIGHT, AND WHAT WENT WRONG, AND HOW CAN WE FIX IT. LET'S DO IT AGAIN.

Exercise

I would be remiss if I didn't discuss exercise as it has related to my life. When I think of exercise, I place it in some other setting rather than a separate category. Each of the paths/interests/ endeavors I have followed in my life mandated a particular regiment of exercise as a part of it. Even now, in my 80s, with the help of my physical therapist, I am creating a new program called, **staying alive and active**. No more heavy weights and low repetitions, now it's less weight, high repetitions, and lots of stretching. My-in the-water time, isn't spent diving now, but rather, doing aquatic exercises in the pool. It's working – I am still alive, and active.

My exercise programs have, at times, been very intense. In the biking section of this book, I talked about how many miles I rode each week. It was a perfect example of specific exercise. The best exercise to do a specific thing, is to do that thing to your maximum ability in practice, so you can reach your maximum+ level in the activity when you need to.

My kayak trip down the Baja coast took the same intensity as my biking program, the exercises, however, were very different. I had a little over one year to get in shape for that trip. I was not in shape for an extreme paddle when the year started. I bought a Concept II rowing machine, and started rowing, and running, to get my general body back in tone. I didn't live near the water, where I could paddle conveniently, so I worked on my general strength for the first few months and only paddled 10 miles once a week. General strength and endurance were my first priority at this stage of my program. My entire program, is spelled out in detail, in the book about that trip, "We Survived Yesterday".

When I moved to Port Ludlow, in Washington, I still had nine months to train. I lived close to the water now and my boat was kept on the dock at the harbor. My training morphed over the next couple of months to 90% paddling.

My new routine was to run to the harbor, one half mile, and paddle as hard as I could, for three to five hours, then run home. My goal was to maintain 4.5 knots for the entire morning. The last month of training, I paddled 14 miles four days a week, (Monday, Tuesday, Wednesday, and Saturday), and 26 miles three days a week, (Thursday, Friday and Sunday), and I could still run home, *I was as ready as I was willing to get.* It proved to be good enough. We paddled 33+ miles a day and the 1,200 miles paddled on the trip was not a problem.

I started the trip at 238 pounds, heavy on purpose, knowing I would need the extra fat to burn on the trip, and the best way to store it was on my body – we didn't have any more room in the boat, it was stuffed to its capacity. I was right, I lost 24 pounds, in 34 days.

The key to all the different exercise programs I have followed during my life has always been, how good did I want to get. I knew I wasn't going to make the effort to be Number One, because that takes about three times the work that it takes to be in the 95 percentiles. I was usually satisfied around the 95 percentiles mark, and generally got bored. It was time to look for something new that would challenge me. A good friend of mine, that I respected very much, gave some words of wisdom that I believe to be true. He said, "If you do the same thing until you are really good at it, which generally takes four to five years, and keep doing it just because it is now simple, you have stopped learning. You should change jobs/activities to something you don't know how to do well so your brain can expand, instead of relaxing". Looking back, that seems to be in line with the way I have spent my life. I believe it to have been the right choice, for me. I have loved my life so far and can't wait to see what is coming next.

I still exercise every day in my new, *stay alive program,* but I must admit, I'm really happy that I don't have to get up at 5am and break the ice off my kayak. Now, I stretch a half hour on my yoga mat on the floor in my warm bed room, get up, make the coffee and sit with my lady to enjoy the start of one more beautiful day of wonder, as we talk about our next adventure.

I still do my floor exercises most every day. They take an hour. I try to get to the gym three times a week, but if I don't make it, it's okay. When we are traveling it's hard to keep up with any program; I just do the best I can. I am happy if I can stay in good shape for the shape I am in. I must admit, however, that sometimes I worry a bit about the shape I'm in. I keep going to my mechanics/doctors and they keep patching me up like an old car. I still run good on surface roads, but I get honked at a lot on the freeways of life. I always get there; it just takes a little longer.

Epilogue

Now I have shared with you the major roads I have taken on my life's journey. All of my endeavors have acted as learning experiences. Some have had more influence than others, but it is all the parts that make the whole, and even the smallest part is necessary to complete the resulting carbon unit, referred to, as a human. Given the genetic blueprint we are born with, we all react to our environment a little differently – this is good, otherwise there would be a very long line we would have to stand in to get the things we want.

Being a teacher, I look at each endeavor as being a semester of investigation into a new topic. I just changed my major more often than most. Like any college major you have to take many courses that are related in substance or interest to the major. More time was spent learning things in my most compelling area of interest at the time, but all of them were needed to get my degree as a happy, productive person.

I think we get our final life degree at the Pearly Gates, when we check in. I hope mine will say, "A Life Well Spent As A Wonderer." I can think of no better way to spend eternity than as a Wonderer, at large, with a universe to wonder about.

I have found that a good life is one of giving. I also have come to realize that to be giving, you have to be living. Taking care of yourself is the most important thing you can do if you want to help others. Many of us put others first, which is easy to do because we love them so much; however, that can lead to having two people that need care instead of just one.

I have had the pleasure of being a caregiver for four different people that I loved very much, for a total of 28 of my 85 years. I don't regret a moment of that time, but I came to realize that I had to keep myself well fed, well exercised, and positive in my thinking, to be able to give them the help they needed.

My advice is – if you have a loved one that needs care, don't hesitate to give it. It will restrict some of the things that you would like to do, but the fact that you are making someone you love as comfortable and well cared for as possible, is a feeling that rises above most everything else. Our worth is gauged by what we can give, not by what we have. When the time comes that you may need help, don't be stubborn. Give someone that loves you the chance to be a giver and feel needed.

A year and a half after my wife of 35 years, Sharon, lost her battle with cancer, I met a widowed lady who is a writer. We found we had a lot in common and over the next few years we have become a couple. We try to travel at least one week a month. During the summer we are generally totally gone for a couple of months to get away from the hot weather.

**NEVER MISS A PARTY OR A TRIP
TO THE GRAND CANYON OR LUNCH ON CATALINA ISLAND**

Karin and I are wonderers, and very positive in our attitude towards life. There is so much to see and learn in this world of ours, that no bucket is big enough to hold the list. We remember back, with much love, but always look forward with anticipation for new places to see, new technology to struggle with, new ideas to test us, new adventures to amaze us and new books to write. Life is such a fantastic gift, we don't want to waste, even a minute of it.

www.ingramcontent.com/pod-product-compliance
Lightning Source LLC
Chambersburg PA
CBHW020428010526
44118CB00010B/468